TIPS for TE
and School Ad

CW01476942

75 articles containing hundreds of effective, practical, easy to follow tips for teachers and school administrators

Written by
Steve Godden and Dan Kehoe.

Cartoons by
Allan Langoulant

Bentley Kehoe Consulting Group

PERTH • AUSTRALIA

First Published 1997.

Published by BKC Pty Ltd
trading as Bentley Kehoe Consulting Group
Suite 3, 108 Stirling Highway, Nedlands,
Western Australia, 6009.

Copyright © 1997 Bentley Kehoe Consulting Group.
ISBN 0646 31151 4

Printed by Lamb Print, Robertson Street,
Perth, Western Australia, 6000

To Order Tips for Teachers
Phone (08) 9389 8098 or Fax (08) 9386 3950.
Discounts Available for Bulk Purchases.

ABOUT THE AUTHORS

Steve Godden is a partner in Bentley Kehoe Consulting Group. Prior to this, he worked as a teacher and school administrator in both Primary and District High Schools throughout Western Australia. In 1994 Steve left teaching to work in the area of Management Consulting and has developed the M•A•P•P™ (Education) System, a process to manage the performance of teachers and school administrators. He has had a great interest in both teacher and leadership development over many years.

Dan Kehoe is the Director of M•A•P•P™ Systems International and Bentley Kehoe Consulting Group. He has worked in the area of organisation development, performance improvement, change management, leadership and adult learning since 1979. He is the designer of the M•A•P•P™ System - a process for improving organisation performance. He is the editor and co-author of "Tips for Managers".

Allan Langoulant is an International Award winning freelance cartoonist and illustrator. He is the recipient of the Walkley Award and has written and illustrated 16 books across a variety of themes. He was also the artist-in-residence at the British International School in Jakarta, Indonesia.

DEDICATIONS

To Debbie, my wife, friend and colleague, the best in all aspects; to my beautiful daughters Brodie and Katie and to all those I have worked with over the last 24 years with the common goal of providing students with the knowledge, skills, attitudes and values that will equip them for life.

Steve Godden

To my mother, Carmel Kehoe, a dedicated and respected educator and administrator.

Dan Kehoe

A special thanks to Carolyn Bodey, our wonderful and highly skilled office manager, colleague and friend who typed and re-typed several copies of the text. Always smiling, totally supportive and never complaining. Our best asset.

Steve and Dan

PREFACE

This book owes its origins to the popular book "Tips for Managers" created and co-written by my "boss", colleague, sparring partner, mentor and fellow 'humorist', Dan Kehoe.

The information in this book is a result of my first hand experience of 21 years of teaching and administration. This period was characterised by frustration, learning, insights, fun, rewards, friendships and immense satisfaction. Teaching was a vocation which I thoroughly enjoyed.

This book identifies key actions which, if performed, will enable both teacher and school administrators to be better at their jobs.

The effectiveness of teachers depends on two things, what they say and what they do. Teaching is an art form and what we have set out to do is translate "art" into action.

We hope that the tips here help you in a practical, no nonsense, down to earth way.

Steve Godden

CONTENTS

WINDOWS TO THE SCHOOL

Assemblies are perhaps the key means by which a school communicates with its community and parent body. Unfortunately many assemblies are a complete waste of time and the damage poorly run assemblies do to a school and staff image is huge.

Parents are a tough audience particularly when the "show" involves their children. There are just three things by which parents make their judgements:

> Can they see?
> Can they hear?
> Do the kids know what they're doing?

Satisfy those three things and you are half way home. You might wish to consider these as a means of improving your assemblies.

☺ Provide time for the students to practise their role in the assembly.

☺ Select items which reflect the ability of the students.

☺ Select items which reflect current teaching topics.

☺ Establish a format for children to follow.

☺ Give children the opportunity to practise speaking with the microphone.

☺ Give children the opportunity to practise speaking in front of an audience.

☺ Ensure that children can be seen during the assembly.

☺ Organise the assembly to fit into the physical setting of the assembly area.

☺ Ensure that the length of the assembly is appropriate to the audience concentration span.

☺ Ensure that the topic/content of the assembly is appropriate to the audience.

☺ Consider cultural differences and understandings when planning the assembly.

☺ Inform parents of when the assembly will be held.

☺ Inform parents of the things the students will need to bring.

☺ Invite parents to attend the assembly.

☺ Ensure children arrive at school earlier than normal on the morning of the assembly.

☺ Ask for parent assistance.

☺ Use existing staff expertise to improve the quality of assemblies.

☺ Appreciate the pleasure that parents get when watching their children perform.

TEACH ME, TEST ME

During the past 20 years there has been a shift in focus from exams to other forms of continuous assessment. At higher levels of education exams still have a part to play. The humble classroom test also. Many argue that they stand as the most valid and reliable means of assessing student performance.

When carrying out any form of assessment there are some crucial elements that have to be considered. Things like marks allocation, format and the degree of difficulty are just some.

When developing assessment tools ensure you maximise their value by giving serious thought to some of these pointers.

☺ Ensure the assessment reflects the objectives of the course being taught.

☺ Prepare different ways of assessing the same concept.

☺ Allocate marks according to the difficulty of concept being assessed.

☺ Discuss the marking key with students.

☺ Discuss the importance of showing any notes or working out.

☺ Avoid having too many similar type examples.

☺ Explain to students the meaning of the phrase "exam technique".

☺ Provide examples of other assessment procedures for students on which they can practise.

☺ Allocate sufficient time for students to be able to complete the assessment task.

☺ Provide reading time before asking students to commence the assessment.

☺ Ask students if they require any clarification of instructions.

☺ Cater for individual abilities within the assessment.

☺ Ensure the assessment is free of spelling, calculation and grammatical errors.

☺ Prepare assessment tasks using word processing software.

☺ Ensure students are given equal opportunity to perform at their best during the assessment process.

☺ Select a venue which is comfortable and has adequate lighting.

☺ Ask questions which test facts and knowledge.

☺ Ask questions which test understanding.

☺ Ask questions which solicit opinion and inference.

☺ Ask questions which explore the appreciative and evaluative aspects of the topic.

YOUR ASSIGNMENT SHOULD YOU CHOOSE TO ACCEPT IT

When we set assignments we do not consider as many issues as we should.

The key purposes for assignments being set are to:

- consolidate prior teaching
- research new work
- develop study habits *and*
- assess knowledge of topic

We need to be very clear about why we are setting the assignment and what our expectations are of the finished product.

To enable students to produce their best work we have to ensure some very basic steps are taken.

☺ Ensure the assignment reflects the objectives of the subject at hand.

☺ Read through the assignment sheet with students.

☺ Ask students if they need any clarification of what is required.

☺ Inform students of presentation expectations.

☺ Allow enough time between setting the assignment and collecting the assignment to enable students to do their best.

☺ Ensure multiple part assignments have each part clearly separated on the assignment sheets.

☺ Inform students of the assessment criteria to be used.

☺ Inform students of the marking key to be used.

☺ Inform students of where information can be located to assist with the assignment.

☺ Provide examples of finished assignments to demonstrate your expectations.

☺ Cover assignment objectives during the normal teaching program.

☺ Word process the assignment sheet.

☺ Provide a list of references.

☺ List the desired learning objectives on the assignment sheet

☺ Discuss your assignment format and content with colleagues for comment

☺ Establish a communication system to inform parents of your expectations and requirements of the student.

'NO THANKS! SCHOOL'S NOT FOR ME."

Schools and gaols are two institutions which have a significant percentage of their 'clients' as reluctant participants.

Like it or not an indicator of the perceived value of what we are offering in education is the number of reluctant students who either do or don't attend school.

Society has changed, as has the family, as has the "power" schools once held. It makes sense to be looking at doing things differently in order to provide a more appropriate and "attractive" learning environment for these students.

Traditional curriculum offerings and teaching methods have failed these students. Schools which are successful at minimising absenteeism look to alternative ways of thinking.

☺ Discuss with colleagues how to establish an environment which is non-threatening to the student.

☺ Prepare work which has an appropriate degree of difficulty and by which students can experience success.

☺ Identify and plan for the specific needs of individuals.

☺ Negotiate a clear set of behavioural expectations.

☺ Learn about the background of students which may influence their decision not to attend school.

☺ Consult with their families to establish consistent expectations.

☺ Take cultural differences into consideration when presenting the learning program.

☺ Encourage students to communicate their thoughts and feelings by holding 'open' discussion sessions.

☺ Work with and use competing interests to encourage students to attend school by building them into the curriculum.

☺ Acknowledge and accept the fact that these students are difficult to manage.

☺ Recognise achievement of results in work attempted.

☺ Recognise effort and movement towards a desired behavioural outcome.

☺ Establish reward systems which recognise achievement and effort in relation to their attendance at school

☺ Identify the specific interests of reluctant students.

☺ Establish learning programs which incorporate the interests of reluctant students.

☺ Acknowledge that, with every new group or individual, the process starts again from the beginning.

☺ Establish performance indicators in relation to the success of the program.

THE TAMING OF THE FEW

The ability of the classroom teacher to effectively manage student behaviour is perhaps the most important skill required to enable a teacher to teach successfully.

Without classroom control very little learning can take place. This frustrates the student wanting to learn and certainly stresses the teacher trying to teach.

The school's Management of Student Behaviour program is regularly revamped and recycled for many reasons. Much time is spent planning, developing, educating staff about and implementing the "new" MSB approach. However little time is spent focussing on the specific actions teachers need to perform to make the program work.

☺ Spend a minimum of 15 minutes per hour teaching time preparing lessons.

☺ Document incidents and your responses to them.

☺ Offer counselling to students who continually misbehave.

☺ Provide counselling to students who continually misbehave.

☺ Inform students about your expectations when they have not complied with a request.

☺ Demonstrate fairness when dealing with unacceptable behaviour.

☺ Demonstrate consistency in dealing with problem students.

☺ Provide realistic consequences to students who demonstrate unacceptable behaviour.

☺ Inform the student's family of serious breaches of rules or persistently bad behaviour.

☺ Inform school administration of unacceptable student behaviour.

☺ Approach unruly students in a calm, non-confrontationist way.

☺ Explain to students the school's and your expectations of student behaviour.

☺ Remain within the constraints of the law.

☺ Seek outside professional help to deal with problem students.

☺ Seek information about the student's current situation which might be causing the problem.

☺ Inform other staff of a problem student's current behaviour.

☺ Comply with the school's MSB policy.

☺ Remind students of rules and expectations on a regular basis.

☺ Provide the opportunity to students to explain the reasons for their behaviour.

☺ Recognise and reward students who demonstrate the required behaviours.

DON'T TEAR YOUR HAIR OUT

One of the toughest challenges for a teacher is dealing with disruptive students during the lesson. How you handle these problems on the spot will influence both your credibility and the degree of respect other students have for you.

Your main goal here is to stop or minimise the disruption which is occurring. If you are seen to act in a way which is both assertive and fair to the student causing the disruption, and to the other students in the class, the situation can generally be managed without too much stress.

It is of vital importance to ensure the recalcitrant student chooses the path of action. You, of course, provide the choices. Depending upon the maturity of your students, the nature of the underlying causes of the student's behaviour and your individual circumstances you may be able to use the following suggestions.

☺ Gain the attention of the disruptive student and ask them if there is a problem.

☺ Ask the student to stop doing what they are doing.

☺ Avoid shouting, losing your temper or arguing the point.

☺ Keep calm and firm throughout the process.

☺ Explain to the rest of the class why you are briefly stopping the lesson to address the problem.

☺ Ask the student if they know what rule they are breaking and what the consequences are of breaking that rule.

☺ Explain the class rule which is being broken by the student and the consequences of breaking that rule.

☺ Ask "How would you like us to proceed now?"

☺ Ask the following types of questions (to appeal to whatever sense of fairness they may have):
  • What effect is your behaviour having on the other students?
  • Do you think what you are doing is fair to the other students?
  • How does what you are doing help you in this situation?

☺ Outline the choices available to both you and the student.
  eg • Stop doing what you are doing, now!
    • Stay behind after school.
    • Go outside for the remainder of the lesson or for the predetermined time.
    • Go and see the person in charge of school discipline.
    • Move to a different part of the classroom.

☺ Ask the student to choose from the options discussed.

☺ Impose the consequence you believe is needed when the student fails to make a choice.

☺ Inform the student that you will meet with them to discuss the problem at a later time.

☺ Repeat the process until it becomes obvious that you now need to exercise your authority.

ARE BULLIES VICTIMS TOO?

Bullying in school has become a pretty hot issue. Many schools have embarked on programs to reduce bullying and to raise awareness about the causes and solutions to prevent bullying.

When we think back on all the "bullies" encountered in our teaching career we realise the common thread is that the environment in which they live models bullying behaviour as the norm. Many bullies are themselves victims.

If you have ever been on the receiving end of a sustained campaign of physical harassment you will know the fear the victim suffers. It has a huge impact on their school and family life and is a problem that must be eradicated.

We must also be aware that it is not just physical intimidation that constitutes bullying.

☺ Discuss the concept of bullying with students.

☺ Engage in educational debate with other staff about bullying.

☺ Read literature related to bullying.

☺ Identify the symptoms and signs of the victim.

☺ Identify the symptoms and signs of the bully.

☺ Discuss the types of bullying that may occur.

☺ Prepare and document a policy on bullying.

☺ Ensure staff are familiar with the policy.

☺ Inform parents of the school community about the school's policy on bullying.

☺ Provide counselling to the bully.

☺ Provide counselling to the victim.

☺ Discuss the consequences of bullying on individuals.

☺ Offer "bully proof" venues for the victims to escape.

☺ Appoint a staff member as a point of contact for the victim.

☺ Inform families of both the bully and the victim of the current situation.

☺ Invite professionals to speak to staff and students about bullying.

☺ Provide counselling to the friends of the bully, the victim and bystanders.

☺ Describe appropriate behaviours for both the bully, the victim and bystanders

☺ Inform them of these behaviours.

☺ Seek home support to reinforce the desired behaviours.

☺ Discuss the consequences of inappropriate behaviour of bystanders.

☺ Provide recognition and reward to both the bully and victim where they demonstrate the desired behaviour.

REMEMBER THE GOOD OLD DAYS

And what, pray tell, gives you the idea that I cannot manage change?

Those who cannot adapt to change will fall by the wayside. As school administrators you need to be accepting of the fact that change is a way of life and that it is your job to facilitate change into schools in the least painful way. That is not to say, that at times, there won't be pain, because there will be.

Gaining staff acceptance of, and commitment to change can be achieved through tapping into their values systems and spending time early in the piece agreeing on the importance of things either happening or not happening. Because people act in accordance with how they perceive things the alignment and broadening of perceptions of staff is an imperative to successfully implementing change.

We can alleviate the fear of the unknown by planning a 'change implementation' strategy.

☺ Consult with staff to be affected by the change before the change is made.

☺ Consult with key stakeholders during the decision making stage.

☺ Discuss with and gain agreement from staff as to why changes are necessary.

☺ Discuss with staff the benefits and likely impact of the proposed change.

☺ Demonstrate support for the intended change.

☺ Question changes if they have been made by people removed from the school.

☺ Ask informed outsiders to talk to staff about the new initiatives.

☺ Prepare an implementation strategy.

☺ Ask staff what they see as the likely impediments to implementing the changes

☺ Involve staff in developing the implementation strategy.

☺ Discuss what needs to be done to implement the agreed changes.

☺ Clarify the roles of yourself and staff once changes are pending.

☺ Review the impact of the change on a regular basis.

☺ Budget for the changes to ensure adequate resourcing.

☺ Inform the parent body of the changes and the reasons behind them.

☺ Be honest when giving reasons for change.

☺ Establish the facts behind rumours and discuss these with staff.

☺ Identify the specific actions which need to be performed during implementation.

☺ Determine a priority order of actions required before implementation.

IS COACHING TEACHING?

Good coaching is an art form and like most things some of us are better at it than others. Years ago coaches used to scream and shout at their players because in those days it was considered to be the way that coaching was done.

These days, fortunately, coaching is about research, analysis, remediation, support, techniques and practise. Good coaches are caring, intelligent, fair and empathetic. They also know their pupil.

In some instances we may be asked to coach a colleague to help them achieve a higher standard. Regardless of who it is the actions are still the same.

☺ Discuss the role of the coach.

☺ • Identify exactly what the person needs to learn. • Set up coaching session. • Tell the person what to do, how to do it and why it is important. • Show them how to do it. • Ask for questions or things to show again. • Get them to practise while you watch. • Give feedback on what they did well and what needs improvement. • Get them to practise again. • Give feedback. • And so on until the person can do it.

☺ Use aids and practical situations to make the coaching session relevant.

☺ Look for opportunities to praise the "trainee".

☺ Use words the trainee understands.

☺ Be honest about your own skills and knowledge.

☺ Allow for discussion when planning a coaching session.

☺ Act to reduce distractions during a coaching session.

☺ Ask the trainee for their knowledge about the area being covered.

☺ Monitor results of coaching in the classroom.

☺ Identify areas still requiring improvement and review where necessary.

☺ Organise and prepare sessions prior to coaching.

☺ Explain the "big picture" and outcomes of the coaching sessions.

☺ Involve the trainee at all times during sessions by encouraging two way communication.

☺ Ask the trainee what they would do differently if a mistake has occurred while they are practising a skill.

☺ Be aware the coaching task is not complete until the objective has been achieved.

☺ Provide a coach who is respected by the trainee.

☺ Act on feedback about your coaching effectiveness immediately.

WHY CAN'T I GET MY MESSAGE THROUGH?

As a school administrator how good are you at communicating? Because something is clear in your mind it may not be clear in the minds of others. We often take for granted that people see things the way we do. The fact is, they don't.

Communication is about informing others about something, and them demonstrating their understanding to the satisfaction of the person sending the message.

In schools there are hundreds of reasons why communication suffers. We all like to know what is going on. Good communication improves job satisfaction and productivity.

- ☺ Explore all the options related to making decisions before communicating to staff.
- ☺ Honestly and forthrightly communicate to staff an unpopular decision.
- ☺ Discuss sensitive issues in a tactful way.
- ☺ Think through the consequences of an issue and the impact it may have on staff.
- ☺ Explain your thoughts about complex issues.
- ☺ Communicate regularly using existing systems and procedures.
- ☺ Seek feedback on key issues.
- ☺ Inform all staff of the school's goals and objectives.
- ☺ Inform all staff of intended changes within the school.
- ☺ Seek clarification from staff to confirm they understand what is required of them.
- ☺ Ask staff to identify the nature and frequency of their communication requirements.
- ☺ Use the most appropriate method to communicate to staff.
- ☺ Document communication systems and procedures in the school.
- ☺ Inform staff of the most correct and appropriate means of communication.
- ☺ Explain what channels of communication staff may use.
- ☺ Ask staff to comply with agreed school communication systems and procedures.
- ☺ Respond to communication from others where a response is appropriate and warranted.
- ☺ Review the effectiveness of your communication skills.
- ☺ Seek feedback on the effectiveness of communication systems and procedures.
- ☺ Seek feedback about your own communication style.
- ☺ Consult with staff about decisions which will affect them before final decisions are made.

THE LIFE BLOOD OF THE SCHOOL

Yes, we're talking about communication, and unfortunately, a topic that has been well and truly "flogged to death".

Understandably so though, because of its perceived importance and the perceived belief that it is **the** major problem in schools and other organisations. Effective communication takes time to establish and implement. However, think of how much time is wasted reworking, correcting, redoing, discussing (rumours) and "bitching" about things because we failed to communicate effectively.

Good communicators establish systems and leave no stone unturned to get the right message across and to ensure that the intent of the message is understood and acknowledged.

☺ Identify where, how and why communication is breaking down.

☺ Discuss with colleagues the nature, format and timing of their individual and work area communication needs.

☺ Consult with other areas to agree your and their communication requirements.

☺ Identify ways to improve communication within your area.

☺ Identify ways to improve communication with other areas.

☺ Attend regular communication sessions with colleagues to allow two-way feedback on any issues important to you and them.

☺ Discuss issues or changes with colleagues as soon as you are aware of them.

☺ Inform school administrators of the nature, format and timing of your own communication requirements.

☺ Cooperate between different departments and sections within the school.

☺ Identify lines of communication within the school which have an internal customer supplier relationship.

☺ Seek information about how the school is performing.

☺ Look for ways to improve the communication systems and procedures.

☺ Seek clarification from colleagues to see that they understand what message is intended or what information is required.

☺ Hold informal communication sessions.

☺ Discuss "grapevine" issues with the school administration and colleagues.

☺ Seek information from school administration on issues about which you are unclear.

LOOK AND LEARN

It is very difficult to present a meaningful learning program if you are not familiar with the environment in which your students live. Teachers, in general, represent mainstream middle class society and our values and standards are different to those of at least 50% of our clientele.

Students appreciate the fact that you 'understand' where they are coming from and the effort that you obviously made to find out. Be careful not to be seen as prying as that can be equally as damaging as it can be good to the whole learning environment. Many home scenarios are the subject of embarrassment and shame so ensure you get 'permission' to discuss their home life.

Empathy is an all powerful communication 'tool' and you cannot empathise until you have actually been there. Here are some ways to find out.

☺ Drive around the streets of the neighbourhood surrounding the school.

☺ Walk around streets surrounding the school.

☺ Talk to students about their home and community.

☺ Engage in discussion with local businesses about the students and the community in general.

☺ Attend community functions.

☺ Meet with community leaders to discuss community issues relevant to the school.

☺ Invite parents and community members to school functions.

☺ Involve the school in community projects.

☺ Initiate and coordinate community projects in which the school can be involved, eg tree planting, tidy town, etc.

☺ Live in the community.

☺ Read local community newspapers and information brochures.

☺ Shop at local community shopping centres.

☺ Organise and lead community activities, eg coaching, committees, etc.

☺ Consider the sensitivity of some home situations.

☺ Avoid being seen as prying.

☺ Seek 'permission' to discuss their home life.

COMPUTERS - FRIEND OR FOE?

Like it or not computers and the related technology are here for good. We cannot allow ourselves or our colleagues to dismiss the importance of this technology.

Using computers as tools to teach with and allowing students access to them for learning prepares them for real life work requirements.

To encourage the use of computers in classes and to develop staff to the level of competence needed to gain maximum benefit from the computer takes money, time and training. We also need to provide an environment which will support the changes needed.

There are many things schools can do to 'tap into technology'.

☺ Appoint a computer education coordinator.

☺ Identify the professional development and training needs of staff.

☺ Budget for the purchase of hardware and software.

☺ Budget for the provision of professional development for staff in hardware and software usage.

☺ Develop a professional development plan.

☺ Use outside sources to educate staff in use of hardware and software.

☺ Encourage staff to purchase their own computers.

☺ Appoint student mentors.

☺ Establish a computer laboratory / technology centre.

☺ Ensure each class has access to a computer in the room.

☺ Plan to use the computer as a teaching tool on a regular basis.

☺ Allocate time showing students and teachers how new software packages work.

☺ Establish a timetable for computer usage.

☺ Seek support from P&C and other fund raising bodies.

☺ Seek donations of hardware and software.

☺ Encourage staff to join computer education associations.

☺ Provide literature about computers in education and related technology.

☺ Discuss with staff why computers in education are important.

☺ Engage in educational debate about computers in education.

☺ Encourage staff to mentor and coach other staff members.

☺ Connect the school to the Internet.

☺ Use computers to communicate with students from other schools.

KIDS HAVE CONFLICTS TOO

If it's hard for adults to cope with conflict and interpersonal crises just imagine how tough it is for children. The great thing about managing conflict, however, is that we can learn significant strategies to control how we react and what we should do when things get too 'hot'.

We must remember the old saying that 'you can't put an old head on young shoulders'. Just as well too when we think about some of the 'old' people we know. Seriously though, life is a great teacher in this area and many people would handle a crisis in their lives far differently should they be given the chance again.

Our role is to facilitate this learning process without too many casualties - emotionally and physically.

☺ Explain the merits of opinions which differed from the student's own.

☺ Demonstrate respect for an opposing point of view.

☺ Consider the interests of all students in conflict when making a decision during the resolution process.

☺ Broaden the students' understanding of a situation by incorporating the different views of others.

☺ Explain the consequences of key decisions on all the conflicting parties.

☺ Encourage a compromise position when both students hold strongly opposing viewpoints.

☺ Encourage students to change their position when they are presented with facts unknown to them.

☺ Describe the conflict situation from the other person's point of view.

☺ Resolve a conflict to the satisfaction of both parties' interests.

☺ Identify a perspective looking at the whole not the parts.

☺ Identify the rights, needs and interests of all students in a conflict situation.

☺ Provide feedback about the student's style or manner in dealing with conflict.

☺ Demonstrate flexibility in your approach to dealing with a conflict of interest.

☺ Encourage the students to concede ground where winning the point would cause more trouble than it's worth.

☺ Consider the dignity and self-respect of the students when attempting to resolve a major problem.

☺ Go out of your way to maintain harmony in a conflict situation.

☺ Discuss issues in neutral territory.

"US" VERSUS "THEM"

Many organisations have an "us" versus "them" mentality. It exists to varying degrees, of course, but is always there lurking in the back of people's minds.

Lack of inter-departmental cooperation can seriously affect the productivity and morale of an organisation.

This is a management function which relates closely to many of the areas presented in "Tips for Teachers". It requires a high degree of consultation before improvements in the area of interdepartmental cooperation can be made.

A great deal of negative energy can be spent in the 'obstructive' mode in schools. Channelling this energy into a positive force ensures that the school becomes a far happier place in which to work.

☺ Identify situations, on a regular basis, which require better cooperation.

☺ Discuss with colleagues the need to improve interdepartmental cooperation.

☺ Identify the causes of poor cooperation between departments.

☺ Ask other department heads how you can assist their department.

☺ Ask colleagues what assistance they require from other departments.

☺ Communicate your cooperation needs and requirements to other departments.

☺ Explain to colleagues the cooperation requirements of other departments.

☺ Ask colleagues what changes are required in the way we operate to improve interdepartmental cooperation.

☺ Ask colleagues how we can implement ways to improve cooperation.

☺ Explain to other department heads what you will be doing to improve interdepartmental cooperation.

☺ Acknowledge the actions of other departments which have responded to your requests for cooperation.

☺ Implement new ways of doing things to improve interdepartmental cooperation.

☺ Provide colleagues with feedback from other departments in relation to any changes they have made.

☺ Provide recognition of individual staff who make efforts to improve interdepartmental cooperation.

☺ Discuss with senior management the actions you require from them to help you improve cooperation.

☺ Implement ways to improve interdepartmental cooperation.

THE KING IS IN HIS COUNTING HOUSE

Keeping the budget under control in all businesses is a challenging task. For the "non-financial" of us there are many unknowns. There are some simple things which we can do to make cost centre management easier and better.

We don't need to be accountants to run effective budget areas. What needs to be considered are things like not buying unnecessary items or getting the best deal.

In this day and age, consultation is a key function of the manager. This is regardless of whether they are managing a cost centre or a staff of a hundred.

☺ Clarify your role as the cost centre manager.

☺ Determine your level of authority and the budget amount that you have to work with.

☺ Consult with other staff as to their needs for your budget area.

☺ Identify items that staff would like purchased.

☺ Develop a priority purchase list.

☺ Confirm that new purchases will not result in duplication of resources.

☺ Follow the school purchasing and ordering procedures.

☺ Prepare a list of items for future budget planning.

☺ Check regularly as to the cost centre situation and expenditure.

☺ Budget for unforeseen items to be purchased by setting aside 10% of your money.

☺ Liaise with the school's financial controller during the management of your cost centre.

☺ Report back to staff regarding the cost centre decisions.

☺ Identify the 'best value' suppliers.

☺ Negotiate best deals and discounts during the purchase.

☺ Report back to Finance Committee about cost centre management decisions regarding purchase requirements.

☺ Comply with the Finance Committee's guidelines and procedures.

☺ Provide the supplier with a valid and current order number.

☺ Carry out monthly reconciliations for your cost centre.

☺ Discuss with colleagues why you decided not to buy items they may have requested and provide the reasons for the decision.

☺ Review your budget every six months.

COUNT EVERY CENT -
EVERY CENT COUNTS

Like every fiscally responsible organisation, schools, at times, need to reduce costs. The school budget is not a bottomless pit which can throw money at everything people want. Responsible cost management must exist.

The trick to reducing costs lies in gaining agreement from all stakeholders that there is firstly a need to do so and secondly that they are willing to implement cost cutting measures.

Part of this process is through consultation with, and the education of, these stakeholders. Here are some fairly simple ways of tackling this great organisational Achilles heel.

☺ Discuss with staff and students about how costs can be reduced.

☺ Identify areas where excessive costs are apparent.

☺ Discuss with stakeholders the need to reduce costs.

☺ Explain to staff and students why cost reduction in an identified area is important.

☺ Establish a strategy and inform all staff and students about how you are going to reduce costs.

☺ Check that the area under review warrants cost reduction.

☺ Implement ways to reduce costs.

☺ Ensure that cost reductions do not result in adverse consequences to either staff or students.

☺ Inform parents of your intentions to reduce costs in the identified area and the reasons why this is happening.

☺ Provide feedback about cost savings to staff and students.

☺ Allocate cost savings to other areas.

☺ Inform staff and students where the saved money will now be spent.

☺ Set targets as to anticipated and expected cost reductions.

☺ Monitor progress and provide feedback to staff and students.

☺ Recognise and reward those who make a concerted effort to reduce costs.

☺ Ensure that cost reductions do not adversely affect the day to day operations of the school.

CHOICES AND CONSEQUENCES

Counselling is about identifying the cause of unacceptable behaviour and setting a course of action to address this cause. In many cases it is not within our sphere of influence to solve the problem but at least we can provide a starting point.

Counselling, if it is to be effective, requires the building of a trusting relationship between the counsellor and the person being counselled.

Just telling somebody not to do something isn't going to have a lasting effect. To get the required behaviour change will require a properly organised support program. To get a sustainable positive behaviour change takes more than most of us are able or willing to do.

☺ Counsel students in private.

☺ Encourage the students to discuss the problems with you.

☺ Ask them where they see the root of the problem to be.

☺ Listen actively by paraphrasing their main points.

☺ Avoid making value judgements.

☺ Refrain from apportioning blame to the cause of the problem.

☺ Explain the consequences of any behaviour in question.

☺ Offer professional advice where you may not be able to help.

☺ Avoid taking sides where a problem involves more than one party.

☺ Separate fact from opinion.

☺ Ask the student for their consent to document issues of a sensitive nature.

☺ Assure the student that the discussions you are holding are confidential.

☺ Ask the student for their consent to inform others should you feel it to be necessary.

☺ Treat all problems as serious regardless of your impressions.

☺ Provide an opportunity for the student to calm down should they be upset.

☺ Encourage students to solve their own problems.

☺ Brainstorm solutions.

☺ Ensure your body language is supportive of their feelings.

☺ Hold discussions in a neutral environment.

☺ Allow the student being counselled to start the conversation.

☺ Provide undivided attention during the counselling process.

A TEMPLATE FOR ALL SUBJECTS

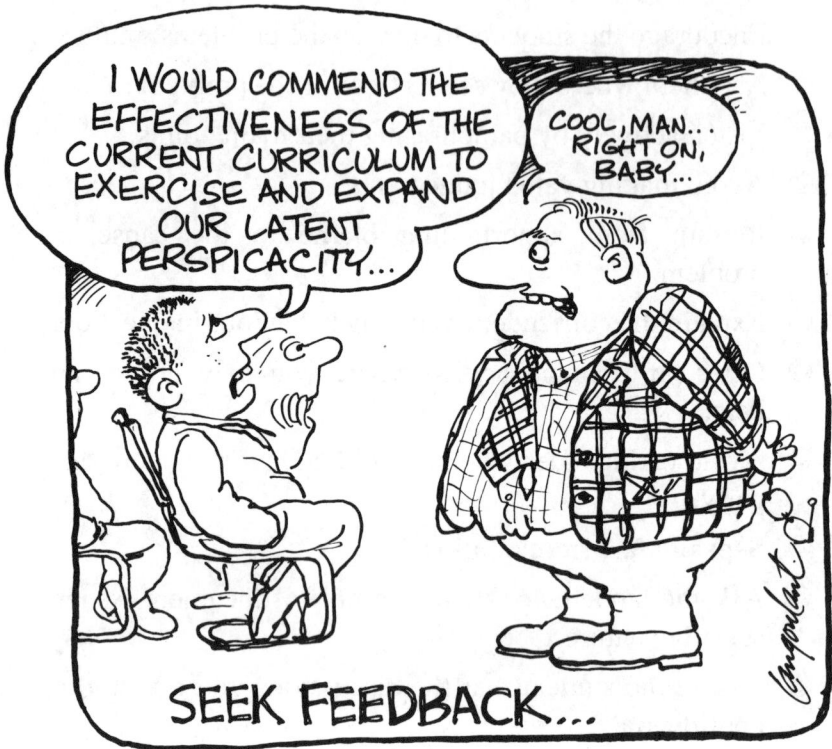

SEEK FEEDBACK....

All curriculum requires a framework for delivery. There are some basic things that need to be done to ensure that the chosen curriculum area gets the support it requires.

It is critical that you, the deliverer, know your subject. Having that "well of knowledge" from which to draw allows you the flexibility of thought to be able to tackle any problem which may arise.

We also need to have a thorough working knowledge of learning styles, developmental learning theory and alternative teaching strategies.

☺ Seek appropriate Professional Development to further develop specific teaching skills in the identified curriculum areas.

☺ Budget for the resourcing of planning, implementation and delivery of the curriculum area.

☺ Seek feedback as to effectiveness of your current curriculum delivery.

☺ Plan together with the school administration to ensure you are clear about school objectives and priorities.

☺ Inform parents of the school's intention to address specific curriculum areas.

☺ Consult with parents to identify the curriculum areas which they consider to be a priority.

☺ Organise the timetable to allow for maximum effectiveness of program delivery.

☺ Seek expertise from outside the school to assist you in the delivery of the curriculum.

☺ Monitor student progress so as to identify areas requiring further emphasis.

☺ Offer your skills to act as the key staff coordinator to assist with the running of the school program.

☺ Develop and use Management Information Systems to assist in measuring the effectiveness of the curriculum delivery.

☺ Monitor student outcomes as a means of measuring the effectiveness of curriculum delivery.

☺ Maintain the delivery and management of curriculum areas which are not high priority focus areas.

☺ Ensure qualified staff are employed with experience in the curriculum area in question.

☺ Discuss with colleagues the benefits of collaborative planning in common curriculum areas.

TEND THE GARDEN - PICK THE FLOWERS

ENCOURAGE STUDENTS TO BRING ITEMS OF INTEREST TO SCHOOL...

How stimulating should a classroom be? What should we put around the room and why? What do we say to the students that will create a positive environment? What is the role of the parent in classroom learning? What can I do and say to reduce student anxieties?

These sorts of questions should lead us to think about what motivates the students to want to learn and what things actually assist them during the learning process.

An environment which is stimulating, collaborative, rewarding, supporting and fun will create a positive learning environment.

☺ Establish learning and interest centres.

☺ Display work samples to demonstrate standards, to recognise performance and effort, and to develop self esteem.

☺ Display charts and learning aids to assist as reference points for student learning.

☺ Arrange classroom furniture to maximise the opportunities for student interaction during learning/ teaching sessions.

☺ Use a variety of teaching activities which promote enthusiasm, participation and interest.

☺ Provide feedback to students during the teaching session which is both meaningful and constructive.

☺ Encourage positive interaction between students.

☺ Acknowledge students who display the types of behaviour you are seeking.

☺ Model the types of behaviour you expect from students.

☺ Involve students in the development of classroom rules.

☺ Discuss with students the classroom rules, routines and procedures and the reasons for them.

☺ Practise established routines and procedures.

☺ Encourage parents to come into the room to see what the students are learning.

☺ Inform parents of the work the students are currently doing and what you intend to cover in the near future.

☺ Request participation from students' family members during classroom activities.

☺ Encourage students to bring items or information of interest to school which is relevant to the current teaching program.

☺ Encourage respect for both people and property.

☺ Ask students to suggest different ways of learning.

THE WORLD IS OUR CLASSROOM

Experience is without doubt the most effective means by which we can learn.

It is naive to think that the best learning can take place within the four walls of a classroom. Seeing, touching, smelling, hearing, discussing and doing outside the classroom provide a far wider variety of learning medium.

It requires enthusiasm, planning and a little extra effort by you and will require that you ensure all stakeholders know exactly what is happening. Follow some of these suggestions when you are organising some outside excursions and you will be well pleased with the learning outcomes achieved.

☺ Establish clear educational objectives related to the excursion.

☺ Ensure the excursion purpose relates to the ongoing school or class program.

☺ Inform parents of time, date, cost, requirements, purpose, transport arrangements etc.

☺ Book transport four weeks ahead of time.

☺ Seek parent assistance on the day.

☺ Visit the excursion venue (where possible) to identify any likely problems and preparation requirements.

☺ Prepare worksheets relevant to the excursion.

☺ Seek parental permission for the students to attend the excursion.

☺ Inform students of any likely dangers.

☺ Establish rules for the excursion and inform all students and adults of these rules.

☺ Check with the school administration to ensure the excursion arrangements, date and venue are O.K.

☺ Carry out a cost analysis before making bookings.

☺ Seek financial support through the school P and C and other agencies.

☺ Confirm that transport is booked one week before the date.

☺ Work in with another class to share the cost.

☺ Check that all students have all their requirements before departing.

☺ Count the students after each activity to ensure they are all there.

☺ Provide a "buddy" for each student during the excursion.

☺ Follow up on the excursion back in the classroom.

☺ Record your preparation details for other staff to use.

☺ Take a mobile phone with you on the excursion.

☺ Discuss the issue of 'Duty of Care'.

GOOD GRIEF!

All schools have situations which result in dissatisfaction for one or other parties. Where a problem situation remains unresolved and one party feels aggrieved it is important that senior management handles the grievance in a fair and objective manner.

One would hope that applying the "grievance policy" is a rarity because the working relationship is often permanently damaged.

In the event that no satisfactory resolution can be found between the parties in conflict, consider these tips to help "knock the issue on the head" once and for all.

- ☺ Establish a school grievance procedure.

- ☺ Familiarise yourself with the school's official grievance procedures.

- ☺ Comply with the established grievance procedure.

- ☺ Ensure all stakeholders have a fair opportunity to state their case.

- ☺ Take union considerations into account.

- ☺ Document the reported grievance and the actions taken to date.

- ☺ Gather all the relevant information.

- ☺ Seek the opinions of staff before making a decision.

- ☺ Brainstorm alternative solutions with the parties in conflict.

- ☺ Make a decision based on fairness and fact and not opinion.

- ☺ Study the impact the grievance may have on the rest of the school.

- ☺ Gain agreement about what the problem is.

- ☺ Gain a commitment from all parties to solve the problem.

- ☺ Negotiate a mutually acceptable solution.

- ☺ Make the necessary decisions to address the grievance.

- ☺ Make provision in the budget to address substantiated grievances.

- ☺ Respect the confidentiality and rights of the complainant.

- ☺ Consider the impact inaction may have on the rest of the staff.

- ☺ Seek advice from colleagues who may be more experienced in grievance handling and resolution processes.

GROUND RULES, OK?

There is little argument that a 'nice' working environment enhances student learning and teacher performance. It rates high in importance for many schools and to do it properly a thorough working plan must be developed which reflects sound architectural, educational, aesthetic, budgetary and environmental practices.

To do this we need to consult with the experts. The cost usually associated with projects of this nature demand that we get it right. Quite often, knowing where to start is the difficult part. Usually the plan or idea is put forward but little happens. Here are some points to consider which may get you off to a flying start.

☺ Establish a grounds committee.

☺ Ensure all key stakeholder groups are represented on the committee.

☺ Carry out a cost analysis.

☺ Seek professional advice and opinion in areas of uncertainty.

☺ Inform parent fundraising bodies of your intended plans.

☺ Consult with stakeholder groups to get their ideas.

☺ Seek funding from external sources to support the project.

☺ Ensure planned changes fit into the existing design and ethos of the school.

☺ Study environmental issues before proceeding.

☺ Inform stakeholders of the benefits of the proposed development.

☺ Consider ongoing maintenance requirements once the improvements have been made.

☺ Draw plans of the proposed development.

☺ Include the school gardener in your planning group.

☺ Seek out hidden costs and problems before commencing.

☺ Use local school and community businesses where possible.

HOME MAKER OR HOME BREAKER?

Homework has a place! No argument.

However, we often take a lot of things for granted and then wonder why the homework isn't done.

Most of us come from a typical middle-class, well-educated background and assume that because **we** have a passion for education and learning, then so should, everyone else. Not so!

Parents can have all the best intentions to ensure homework is completed but for a variety of reasons may have difficulty making it happen.

- ☺ Establish a recording system for students to write out what homework they have to complete.
- ☺ Establish a communication procedure which informs parents of set homework.
- ☺ Set realistic completion times.
- ☺ Set amounts of homework which can be realistically completed.
- ☺ Explain the requirements and objectives of the homework.
- ☺ Set homework which is relevant to the current curriculum being taught.
- ☺ Discuss with students your expectations regarding the standards, format and methodology required.
- ☺ Document, for parents and students, your expectations of the standards, format and methodology required.
- ☺ Inform students of their responsibilities.
- ☺ Inform parents of their responsibilities.
- ☺ Inform parents and students of your responsibilities.
- ☺ Comply with the school's homework policy.
- ☺ Follow up with students who have not completed their homework.
- ☺ Allow students to stay back at school to complete their homework if the home environment is a problem.
- ☺ Cater for the needs of students to have time to play/recreate after school.
- ☺ Discuss with parents the importance of playing.
- ☺ Mark all homework and provide feedback to students.
- ☺ Set homework which has been covered in the course of the normal teaching program.
- ☺ Set homework which is designed as research for a new topic.

FIRST IMPRESSIONS STICK

Too often when new teachers arrive in a school they are left to fend for themselves. A simple tour around the school is not good enough for their orientation.

Inducting new staff properly can result in greater productivity earlier, enhance workplace satisfaction for them and enable them to fit into the team more quickly and easily.

Someone needs to assume responsibility for the induction of new staff into the school. The new teacher will be far happier if the person carrying out the induction follows these tips.

☺ Introduce the new staff member to teaching staff with whom they will be working near or with.

☺ Introduce them to all school administrative members.

☺ Introduce them to all non-teaching staff.

☺ Welcome the new staff member publicly.

☺ Arrange for a guided tour of the school.

☺ Explain the basic vital ways things are done at your school, eg duty, messages, leave, security, resource borrowing, etc.

☺ Prepare an induction plan.

☺ Provide a "buddy" for the new staff member.

☺ Demonstrate how to use school equipment, eg phone, photocopier, fax , binding machine, etc.

☺ Show them where **all** resources are kept.

☺ Provide a key to their teaching area.

☺ Discuss issues unique to the school environment and clientele.

☺ Provide them with important contact numbers, eg District Office, yours, school, Education Department, etc.

☺ Provide them with a timetable of school 'events' which occur on a regular basis, eg assemblies, newsletters, staff meetings, etc.

☺ Discuss school development priorities.

☺ Provide time for the inductee to absorb the information they have been given.

☺ Set aside time for the staff member to ask questions after they've been at the school for two weeks.

☺ Inform them of the normal communication procedures.

EXCUSE ME? CAN YOU HELP ME?
I'M NEW HERE.

Any time we come into an environment with which we are unfamiliar elements of uncertainty and anxiety will exist. Students who are new to a school environment have enough emotional traumas to cope with without having to wonder 'who'? or 'what'? or 'when?' or 'where'?

To enable them to slot into the learning program quickly and without added distraction, the school must have some induction strategy in place.

Induction means providing information about the location of key areas, introductions, descriptions of routines and procedures and the giving of reasons why.

☺ Appoint a buddy

☺ Appoint a staff member as a contact point.

☺ Provide them with their current timetable

☺ Introduce them and their parents to their new teacher/s

☺ Provide a map of the school

☺ Show them the rooms in which they will be working

☺ Give them a guided tour of the school and its facilities

☺ Explain the school dress code and the minimum standards

☺ Explain the school rules and regulations and the expectations of students

☺ Provide an opportunity for them to ask questions

☺ Introduce them to other staff members of importance e.g. school psych, nurse, police, registrar etc

☺ Follow up regularly to ensure they are coping - fortnightly initially

☺ Match the curriculum areas they studied at their previous school to those which exist at their new school

☺ Contact the family to check that they are settling in

☺ Provide them with a current booklist and equipment they may need.

☺ Explain school book renting or borrowing procedures.

READ MY MIND

How often do we issue instructions to students and think that the message is clear only to find that half the class haven't a clue about what it is we have asked them to do?

We take for granted that because its clear in our mind it should also be clear in the minds of the students.

Next time you issue instructions and get a response which is not what you were expecting ask yourself - "Is it me? Or "Is it them?" Either way there may be some simple things you are not doing.

☺ Choose a venue which enables students to hear and see what it is that you want them to do.

☺ Ensure you can be seen by all students.

☺ Ensure you can see all students.

☺ Ensure all students can hear you when you issue instructions.

☺ Choose a venue which is free from distractions.

☺ Ensure students are giving their undivided attention when instructions are issued.

☺ Write your instructions as a step by step process.

☺ Stop talking while students are reading instructions.

☺ Outline what it is you want the students to do at each step.

☺ Break the instruction up into a 'step by step' format where the instructions are long. Check understanding of each step.

☺ Demonstrate what it is you want the students to do.

☺ Seek feedback from students to ensure instructions are fully understood.

☺ Present instructions in manageable portions to ensure maximum understanding of what is required.

☺ Provide written support materials for later reference.

☺ Ask the students to demonstrate that they understand what the instructions mean.

☺ Provide opportunities for students to learn to practise following instructions.

☺ Encourage students to ask questions where they are unsure of what is required.

☺ Ask questions of students to gauge their level of understanding.

DEALING AND COPING WITH PERSONALITY CLASHES

When groups of people are together for long periods of time, it is inevitable that there will be clashes. How we deal with personality clashes is all important for the maintenance of harmony, motivation and productivity.

Realising and understanding that because someone doesn't do things the way we would like them done or doesn't agree with our point of view doesn't necessarily mean that they are wrong.

We draw on the ability to make decisions and form opinions from all the factors which shape our lives. Background, upbringing, culture, age, gender, religion, experiences, education, opportunity, luck, all influence how we think. These factors influence how we perceive things and we respond and act according to our perceptions.

☺ Consider the merits of opinions which differ from yours.

☺ Demonstrate respect for an opposing point of view.

☺ Discuss the for and against for both points of view.

☺ Seek assistance from colleagues to act as mediators.

☺ Consider the interests of, and consequences on, all stakeholders when decisions are made.

☺ Adopt a compromise position when both parties hold strongly opposing viewpoints.

☺ Change your position when you are presented with facts unknown to you.

☺ Describe a conflict situation from the other person's point of view.

☺ Check to see that the other party is satisfied after a resolution has been reached.

☺ Identify the right, needs and interests of all parties in a conflict situation.

☺ Ask for and receive feedback about your own style or manner.

☺ Concede ground because to win the point would cause more trouble than it's worth.

☺ Avoid saying things which may damage the dignity and self-respect of others.

☺ Stop the conversation and suggest another time to continue when tempers 'flare'.

☺ Focus on the issue and not the person.

☺ Agree that you will act to solve any points of disagreement.

☺ Agree that an issue is finished with once a decision is made.

☺ Avoid 'clouding' work issues with unassociated problems.

☺ Seek professional advice where you find you are in conflict with many people about many issues.

☺ Ask yourself "what are the consequences if I concede the point?"

☺ Hold discussions when your mind is fresh and clear - not tired.

READIN' AND 'RITIN' - THERE EVERYWHERE

What was your initial reaction to the heading of this topic? Mild embarrassment, contempt for the authors, you didn't notice.... Whatever it was, the misspelling of 'they're' can highlight how literacy skills, or lack there of, are used to assess the effectiveness of a person's schooling and level of intellect.

It is the responsibility of all curriculum areas to aim to ensure literacy levels are constantly being lifted. Literacy is about providing the skills and strategies to enable students to glean maximum learning from **any** written content that might be presented and present back these learnings in the most effective way.

All too often we fail to realise that every subject area is a small, but important part of the big literacy ' picture'.

☺ Seek appropriate Professional Development to develop specific skills in the literacy area.

☺ Use teaching strategies which assist students to gain meaning from written materials.

☺ Teach strategies to students which allow them to gain meaning from written materials.

☺ Discuss with colleagues the importance of literacy to students.

☺ Establish a literacy resource area for each subject.

☺ Provide documentation/literature about literacy to staff.

☺ Identify key objectives needed for the improvement of literacy.

☺ Encourage staff to experiment with teaching strategies with a literacy focus.

☺ Appoint a literacy coordinator.

☺ Write sample lesson plans for each subject area.

☺ Prepare a literacy improvement timeline for implementation of teaching strategies.

☺ Identify literacy skills which are needed in each subject area.

☺ Share learning strategies with other staff.

☺ Purchase curriculum materials which have a literacy focus, eg science, social studies.

☺ Establish clear literacy outcomes for each subject area.

☺ Discuss with staff the concept of developmental learning.

☺ Discuss with colleagues from other subject areas what you are doing to develop literacy levels.

☺ Identify students who have specific literacy development needs.

FACT OR FICTION?

SEEK STAFF OPINIONS ON RESULTS

Identifying "problem" areas which need addressing is usually left to a "gut feeling" or "professional judgement". These days this is just not enough on its own. There needs to be verifiable evidence that a problem area exists and that we need to allocate our time and energies in this direction.

This is all part of the accountability process which ensures we don't waste our time, energy and money.

Management Information Systems are a means by which we gather data and collect information which in turn enable us, through analysis, to determine the status of the area under review.

- ☺ Discuss with staff what Management Information Systems are.
- ☺ Discuss with staff the benefits to the school of using Management Information Systems.
- ☺ Present alternative means of gathering information.
- ☺ Discuss and agree with staff the best means of gathering information.
- ☺ Identify the curriculum areas for which information will be required.
- ☺ Train staff in how to gather the information, eg use and analyse standardised tests.
- ☺ Identify year level groups for which information will be gathered.
- ☺ Analyse the results to determine the standards within the group.
- ☺ Prepare reports which provide evidence of results.
- ☺ Seek staff opinions on results.
- ☺ Express results in a graphical format.
- ☺ Display results for staff to consult and discuss.
- ☺ Discuss the results with staff.
- ☺ Identify the specific needs of individuals within the groups.
- ☺ Prepare a plan to address the needs of special groups.
- ☺ Resource the plan according to need and current school priority.
- ☺ Keep records of all data collected and decisions made.
- ☺ Compare the information collected against the school's performance indicators.
- ☺ Define and discuss the key performance areas in the school.
- ☺ Agree with stakeholders the key performance indicators.

RIGHT OR WRONG - WHO CARES?

I'LL GIVE YOU BETTER MARKS, SAMANTHA, IF YOU CAN TELL ME MORE ABOUT CAPTAIN COOK....SO FAR YOU'VE SAID HE WAS A SPUNKY HUNK."

Marking work is an extremely powerful way to inform students about their progress. The sooner the feedback and the more detailed the feedback the greater the learning takes place.

Marking work, like record keeping, must be functional and purposeful. Marking ranks high on the list of things crucial to effective teaching.

We need to consider when and where we mark, marking scales and values and how these are communicated to the student and family.

- ☺ Provide feedback to students which identifies points of error by showing correct answers and / or working out.
- ☺ Use a marking colour which is easily distinguished eg red.
- ☺ Demonstrate work which is of an acceptable standard early in the lesson and explain why it is acceptable.
- ☺ Use other aids to assist with marking eg stickers, comments, rewards etc.
- ☺ Check and mark **all** work that students produce.
- ☺ Establish a clear criteria for your marking key and explain how it works to students.
- ☺ Allocate "part" marks for work where only partial understanding is demonstrated.
- ☺ Record all your marks in the agreed format.
- ☺ Use your marks to assist with reporting to parents.
- ☺ Choose a method of marking work that provides meaningful feedback to the student and parents.
- ☺ Mark work as a means of consolidating a teaching concept.
- ☺ Allow students the opportunity to produce the highest standard possible before marking.
- ☺ Avoid embarrassing students when informing them of their results whether these results are good or bad.
- ☺ Move around the room for "over the shoulder" marking when students have been given set work.
- ☺ Establish and use a consistent marking key to allow students to place a "value" to the mark.
- ☺ Negotiate a collection time and return date for marked work.
- ☺ Explain the penalties for late work.
- ☺ Explain why student work has not been marked if you fail to mark in the agreed time.
- ☺ Know your subject content and the correct answers.
- ☺ Ensure uniformity of marking scale, across a year level or faculty group.
- ☺ Look for opportunities to reinforce right efforts even if the results aren't up to standard.

MEETINGS, MEETINGS, MEETINGS

Many meetings are a waste of time! If the best decisions are not made in a time frame which is reasonable it is due to one of these things:

- poor meeting structure
- poor leadership *or*
- poor participation

As the chairperson and participant we have responsibilities before, during and after the meeting.

Meetings represent the best available consultation process for maximising effectiveness and improving school productivity.

☺ Prior to the meeting, circulate its objectives and the input required from participants.

☺ Set a time limit on the meetings duration.

☺ Start the meeting on time, even if some people aren't present.

☺ End the meeting on time, regardless of whether objectives are achieved.

☺ Limit the number of objectives to those that can be achieved within the time available.

☺ Estimate the amount of time needed to discuss each objective.

☺ Plan ways of making the meeting interesting by using aids, charts, transparencies, activities, etc.

☺ Ensure aids such as overhead projectors are working before the meeting starts.

☺ Control the discussion by nominating who is to talk, and when.

☺ Open the meeting by clarifying objectives, format and expectations.

☺ Appoint someone to record the key points and decisions reached during the meeting.

☺ Rotate the leadership role so that other people develop the confidence and competence to conduct effective meetings.

☺ Encourage participation by ensuring that every person's contribution is heard.

☺ Ask questions of non-contributors.

☺ Ensure that all discussion is relevant to the stated objectives.

☺ Ask talkative members to clarify how their comments relate to the objectives.

☺ Prepare an "action plan" sheet for each person's use.

☺ Record on the action plans who does what, how and by when, etc.

... AND MORE BLOODY MEETINGS

One of the interesting things about the nature of teachers is that they are generally very strong in their beliefs about issues. The staff meeting is the official forum at which these issues can be 'aired'. Because of the nature of education and the contentious issues that often arise we need to ensure that the time spent during staff meetings is not wasted.

☺ Spend time discussing ways to make meetings more valuable (not during the meeting).

☺ Inform participants in written form, of meeting details, such as time, venue and agenda.

☺ Select a time of the day to hold the meeting that allows participants to give their undivided attention.

☺ Counsel disruptive participants after the meeting pointing out the consequences of their actions on the meeting.

☺ Ensure you are prepared in the areas for which you are responsible.

☺ Think through the issues likely to be raised and plan your contribution.

☺ Follow up on agreed actions with staff responsible for completing that action.

☺ Encourage consensus when making decisions.

☺ Focus on facts more than opinions.

☺ Summarise the key points of a discussion to ensure clarity of issue and decision.

☺ Prepare an appropriate agenda.

☺ Provide opportunities for all colleagues to contribute to the agenda.

☺ Make "hidden agendas" the subject of a separate meeting.

☺ Ensure all colleagues have the opportunity to participate in the meeting.

☺ Conduct the meeting according to standard meeting conventions.

☺ Record the minutes of the meeting.

☺ Meet regularly with colleagues.

☺ Agree with colleagues the amount of time needed to conduct the staff meeting.

A VOYAGE OF SELF DISCOVERY

The concept of mentoring is one which is becoming a more accepted form of peer development. The art of mentoring requires a subtle approach and is generally not well done. Mentoring allows the learner to learn by experiencing the consequences of their own actions.

Effective mentoring relies heavily on the ability of the mentor to guide the learner to take control of their own learning.

It is a process of self discovery and insight for the learner and, to a lesser degree, the mentor.

☺ Allow time for the learner to develop - move at their pace.

☺ Assess what the learner knows - don't assume they know.

☺ Use "identification" by describing how you felt in a similar situation - use empathy.

☺ Focus on putting the person at ease early in the process.

☺ Avoid accepting generalisations as answers to questions.

☺ Tolerate mistakes - use them as opportunities to learn.

☺ Conduct mentoring on their territory.

☺ Avoid discounting their ideas - use them to springboard into other ways of thinking.

☺ Focus on using questions which require the learner to show understanding.

☺ Use hypothetical situations - "If ... what would you do?"

☺ Determine the problem before moving to resolutions.

☺ Recognise the different realities of the learner - their perception may differ from yours.

☺ Be aware of not over assisting.

☺ Allocate appropriate time for mentoring.

☺ Hold a meeting to establish and write purpose, process, conditions and desired outcomes.

☺ Clarify the roles and responsibilities of mentor and learner.

☺ Let the learner decide and act on their decision.

☺ Focus on improvement - not change - new, different and better.

☺ Create an information file to assist the process.

☺ Focus on getting the learner talking rather than you talking.

☺ Ask questions which show the learner that you are curious about the answer / solution and avoid "you should" statements.

☺ Acknowledge your shortfalls in knowledge / experience of the mentoring process.

☺ Point out learner's strengths.

☺ Seek permission to give advice.

THE FORCE WITHIN

You cannot force people do anything they don't want to do. History is full of examples of people who resist bowing to pressure to do things in a way that does not suit them.

If we can motivate staff to do the things which we believe are important to the school and important to teaching, our job becomes much easier.

Motivation is not about tricking people into doing things. It is about them wanting to do something because they value and perceive that action to be important.

A simple statement from Abraham Lincoln nicely sums up the situation; " A person convinced against his will is of the same opinion still."

☺ Involve staff in goal setting, planning and decision making.

☺ Let staff know that their opinion is valued.

☺ Use the ideas and suggestions of staff and give them recognition and credit.

☺ Involve staff in discussions about planned changes and in particular things which affect their job.

☺ Inform staff of the big picture and how staff contribute towards school goals.

☺ Model the required behaviours and standards to others that you expect of them.

☺ Make regular positive comments about the school to staff.

☺ Delegate to staff where they are willing and able to take on tasks.

☺ Check that you are seen by staff as decisive, consistent and fair in the way you do things.

☺ Clarify goals, individual roles, standards of performance and expectations of staff.

☺ Offer regular recognition and feedback about staff performance particularly where staff are doing well.

☺ Ask staff about how their motivation could be improved.

☺ Offer support to staff who may be having difficulty in performing tasks.

☺ Be seen to act to address poor job performance or sub-standard work.

☺ Agree with staff a step by step performance counselling process.

☺ Counsel people in private when dealing with poor performance.

☺ Get staff together and identify their problems, needs and concerns.

☺ Allow a degree of flexibility and choice about how staff achieve their objectives.

YOU CAN LEAD A HORSE TO WATER

Student motivation to a certain extent rests with the students themselves. However, we can influence their desire to learn by applying some simple principles.

When was the last time you seriously considered how you would motivate the students in your subject area? Telling them they have to do it "Because I said so!" doesn't hold with a lot of students or adults for that matter.

It appears that student motivation drops away dramatically after the first 3-4 years of school. It tends to pick up towards the latter years, though this can be more through a fear of failure than really wanting to be there to learn.

☺ Involve students in goal setting, planning and decision making.

☺ Tell students what they are doing well.

☺ Let students know that their opinion is valued.

☺ Use the ideas and suggestions of students and give them recognition and credit.

☺ Involve students in discussions about planned changes and in particular things which affect their school life.

☺ Model the required behaviours and standards to students that you expect of them.

☺ Make regular positive comments about the school to students.

☺ Delegate to students where they are willing and able to take on tasks.

☺ Check that you are seen by students as decisive, consistent and fair in the way you do things.

☺ Clarify objectives, individual roles, standards of performance and expectations of students.

☺ Offer regular recognition and feedback about student performance.

☺ Ask students about what things they could do to improve their motivation.

☺ Offer support to students who may be having difficulty in performing tasks.

☺ Provide counselling to students who are not performing to the agreed standard.

☺ Counsel students in private when dealing with poor performance.

☺ Seek student's ideas before making a key decision which will affect their class or subject area.

☺ Communicate the problems and concerns of students to other staff members.

☺ Demonstrate visible staff support by asking students what can be done to help them.

EXTRA, EXTRA ...
READ ALL ABOUT IT ...

Just how many school newsletters get home is one question and how many get read is another. Whatever the answer, their main purpose is to act as a communication medium between the school and the home.

In this day and age of word processors, the quality of production of newsletters has improved immensely compared to what it was when they first rolled off the 'press'. However their effectiveness, in many cases, remains unchanged.

We need to consider how often they should go out, what should go in them, how to get them home and how to ensure they are read. Each impacts on the effectiveness of the other. Remember if they are meant to be read then make them readable.

☺ Provide a calendar of events for the term.

☺ Establish a consistent format and size.

☺ Ensure the print size is readable (12pt or more).

☺ Utilise the word processing facilities of your computer to enhance the presentation.

☺ Report school happenings, events and concerns.

☺ Use the newsletter to publicly acknowledge and thank people who have contributed to the school.

☺ Advertise community events and activities.

☺ Use the newsletter to display student work.

☺ Produce newsletters weekly.

☺ Allow for differing literacy levels by using simple language.

☺ Avoid using education jargon and acronyms.

☺ Produce newsletters in languages other than English which may be predominant in the school.

☺ Provide all staff with their own copy.

☺ Ensure staff distribute newsletters on time.

☺ Edit text and check all dates before printing newsletters.

☺ Seek feedback from the school community about ways of improving the newsletter.

☺ Establish a regular distribution system.

☺ Use coloured paper as a means of recognising the newsletter.

IT'S ALL A NUMBERS GAME

Numeracy is one of the three "Rs" or in other words is one of the three ways society measures a successful education. This is because numeracy skills, or lack there of, are easily observed and measured.

As educators we often fail to take a holistic view of numeracy. We tend to think it lies within the domain of mathematics and mathematics alone. This is a false assumption and it needs to be understood that **all** subjects have a numeracy component. (English included).

The importance of numeracy should not be underestimated and we must strive to ensure that all students are functionally numerate when they leave school. This means they have the basic skills to make them both employable and self sufficient.

- ☺ Appoint a school numeracy coordinator.
- ☺ Discuss and define the meaning of numeracy.
- ☺ Establish a numeracy resource area.
- ☺ Discuss with colleagues the importance of numeracy.
- ☺ Identify and document objectives in other subjects which relate to numeracy.
- ☺ Discuss with colleagues the areas in which numeracy can be found other than in mathematics.
- ☺ Prepare numeracy sessions which relate to these other subjects.
- ☺ Budget for resources to support the numeracy program.
- ☺ Purchase literature which relates to the teaching of numeracy.
- ☺ Identify the bottom line basics that students need to know in relation to numeracy and life after school.
- ☺ Ensure staff understand the terms "concrete", "pictorial" and "abstract" in relation to numeracy.
- ☺ Discuss with colleagues the concept of developmental learning.
- ☺ Discuss with colleagues the concept of learning style in relation to numeracy.
- ☺ Plan numeracy learning activities in which students can participate.
- ☺ Ask more competent staff members to act as mentors or coaches to colleagues.
- ☺ Identify and provide for the professional development needs of staff in relation to numeracy.
- ☺ Establish clear numeracy outcomes in each subject area.
- ☺ Seek professional development in the area of numeracy.

IF YOU DON'T KNOW WHERE YOU'RE GOING, IT DOESN'T MATTER HOW YOU GET THERE

Objectives, goals, aims, ... call them what you like, they all mean the same thing. They describe what it is that we intend to do. Some are broader in scope than others and some have more specific intentions but they all still come back to one thing - **purpose**.

If we are clear about what it is we intend to do, the planning phase follows naturally. Dare it be said that at times we teach for content first and then consider what the real objective of the exercise was later (if at all).

It is of paramount importance to have a clear vision about what you wish to achieve before embarking on the difficult task of getting there. Unless, of course, you enjoy surprises.

☺ Ensure staff are aware of the Mission / Purpose statements of the school.

☺ Identify key Outcome Areas requiring direction.

☺ Ensure objectives are concise and unambiguous.

☺ Specify a single key result to be achieved.

☺ Specify only the what and when.

☺ Check that staff understand what the objective means.

☺ Ensure objectives are challenging and realistic.

☺ Ensure that the objectives fit into school policies and practices.

☺ Consult with other stakeholders during the development of goals and objectives.

☺ Document goals and objectives.

☺ Ensure the goals and objectives identified can be resourced.

☺ Discuss with staff how their job fits into the organisational goals of the school.

☺ Discuss with staff the major things they are expected to achieve through their teaching.

☺ Identify where school development priorities lie.

☺ Identify the key tasks, jobs and functions which will have to be performed to address the priority areas.

☺ Check to see if the school's goals and your teaching goals are going to meet the needs of the students.

☺ Provide a budget which will support the goals and objectives of the school program.

☺ Identify key performance indicators.

☺ Prepare a timeline which outlines when key performance indicators should be met.

GUESS WHICH HAND IT'S IN

Just like teachers parents are busy people too. To maximise the understanding of any intended message you need to consider many things. This chapter has been written from the perspective of what a parent needs.

There is no doubt that if you are effective as a communicator the relationship between you and the family is positive. Most parents like to know what is going on but more importantly why things happen and why some decisions are made.

Clear communication can reduce the number of "bush fires" that often occur because of uncertainty about what is happening. It also helps to reduce any uninformed rumour or gossip.

- ☺ Report on the student's progress to parents on a regular basis.
- ☺ Hold interviews with parents to review student progress.
- ☺ Alert parents as to forthcoming activities.
- ☺ Inform parents of likely expenses related to class and school activities.
- ☺ Inform parents of the likely course content, key objectives and assessment procedures and methods you will be adopting.
- ☺ Inform parents of changes to class, school and department policy.
- ☺ Allow parents the opportunity to respond to any communication you may initiate.
- ☺ Cater for the literacy levels of parents during written communication.
- ☺ Allow for cultural differences during the communication process.
- ☺ Establish regular communication systems and procedures with parents.
- ☺ Respond promptly to parent requests or concerns.
- ☺ Send home school/class/faculty newsletters.
- ☺ Hold regular parent meetings as communication sessions.
- ☺ Monitor that information has reached parents.
- ☺ Check to see that school newsletters are taken home on time.
- ☺ Read school newsletters to familiarise yourself with the content.
- ☺ Follow the school's communication procedures.
- ☺ Consider emotional issues when communicating about sensitive matters such as discipline.
- ☺ Keep a record of all communication to parents.
- ☺ Ask parents what information they need to know.

PARENTS AS PARTNERS

Parents can be a great ally or a terrible enemy. Many parents are keen to assist in the school program and possess some fantastic abilities. To use the expertise and enthusiasm of the parent body can enhance the education program dramatically.

You should, of course, ensure that their motives for participation in the classroom are correct before inviting them to help.

A positive partnership between school and family has a huge impact on the student's learning and self worth. If students see their parents working towards helping the school achieve its goals they will more willingly become involved themselves.

☺ Inform parents of school activities to provide them with the opportunity to participate in areas of interest.

☺ Seek feedback from parents as to their impressions and opinions about school programs.

☺ Provide a forum for parents to contribute to school policy and planning priorities.

☺ Encourage parents to become partners in the learning process by inviting them into class rooms.

☺ Encourage parents to involve themselves in the education debate so as to increase their understanding of issues.

☺ Respond to parent suggestions about school programs about which they may not agree.

☺ Keep a balance between the expectations of the education officialdom and parents demands.

☺ Acknowledge, in public, parent contributions which have enhanced the school learning program.

☺ Assess the value that individual parents can offer to a school program.

☺ Consider the 'vested interests' of individual parents when allowing them to participate in the school program.

☺ Identify and use the individual abilities parents may have that can enhance the school program.

☺ Encourage parents to involve themselves with School Councils, P&C Groups, etc.

☺ Tolerate views that parents may have that may be different to your own.

☺ Develop a data base of parents' occupations, skills and interests.

TWO HEADS ARE BETTER THAN ONE

During any decision making process the combined power of the group will always exceed the sum of the powers of the individuals making up the group. Planning together has some huge benefits for all involved in the process. The learning gained and the time that can be saved are but two of them.

Collaboration is about giving and receiving, sharing, listening, discussing and making decisions together. We can tap into the well of knowledge which often sits wasted in schools, if we adopt a collaborative planning strategy.

- ☺ Discuss and agree the purpose and intended outcomes of the collaborative planning exercise.
- ☺ Determine which teachers will form the collaborative planning team.
- ☺ Agree a team coordinator.
- ☺ Discuss with team members the benefits of collaborative planning.
- ☺ Identify and agree the subjects or areas around which collaborative planning will happen.
- ☺ Identify and agree the role and responsibilities of team members and the coordinator.
- ☺ Establish and document a schedule, the frequency and venue of meetings.
- ☺ Discuss, identify and use the strengths and experience of all team members.
- ☺ Discuss and identify the needs of the students.
- ☺ Seek information from others who are already successfully planning collaboratively.
- ☺ Observe other planning teams in action.
- ☺ Prepare an agenda for planning meetings.
- ☺ Discuss and agree the roles of the class, subject, support and specialist teachers in the collaboration process.
- ☺ Discuss and agree the teaching strategies and resources to be used during lessons.
- ☺ Discuss and seek agreement that the provision of support teaching time is for the direct benefit of the students.
- ☺ Discuss with and inform parents about what collaborative planning is and how the students will benefit.
- ☺ Review the progress of the planning process regularly.
- ☺ Discuss ways to improve the planning process once a review has been undertaken.
- ☺ Discuss with school administration what they need to do to support the collaborative planning process.
- ☺ Report back to the school administration about your results.

THINGS TO DO IN YOUR
SCHOOL HOLIDAYS

All good teachers plan what they are going to teach. It is generally recommended that we document our plans. But what should we document?

There are many teachers who work on the philosophy of "teaching by immersion" and hoping that some things will stick. There is no doubt that this process has a small place but it must be complemented with some framework which identifies intended outcomes and stated objectives.

Planning can be a chore, a bit like preparing a room before painting it. If we don't do the preparatory things then the finished product is not as good.

☺ Structure a clear sequence of content related to the knowledge and skills you want to impart.

☺ Plan learning activities which enhance your teaching.

☺ Use existing resources to assist with the learning activities you may wish to present.

☺ Identify specific curriculum areas in your planning program.

☺ Document your plans clearly outlining the objectives, teaching strategies, evaluation procedures and resources.

☺ Identify specific classroom management areas which require planning.

☺ Encompass school priorities into your planning.

☺ Cater for abilities and developmental stages of your students.

☺ Discuss with colleagues ways of improving planning.

☺ Comply with agreed documentation procedures during planning methods.

☺ Prepare an overview of what it is you intend to teach.

☺ Plan your teaching in set time blocks.

☺ Consider the needs of all subjects when planning.

☺ Prepare and document a timetable of subjects to be taught.

☺ Discuss your plans with your colleagues and school administration.

☺ Use subject overviews to assist with planning.

☺ Submit an overview of your plan to the school administration.

SUCCESS IS NO ACCIDENT ...
YOU HAVE TO PREPARE FOR IT

ANTICIPATE THE LIKELY PROBLEMS WHICH MAY ARISE.

Effective preparation is crucial to effective teaching. There are two things which lessen the effectiveness of teaching - under-preparation and over-preparation. As with most things we need to keep a balance.

The more experienced teacher probably expects to spend less time preparing because the structure and pitfalls of the lesson are well known to them. Because of this experience it can, however, lead us into a sense of complacency, and more importantly limit our effectiveness.

The less experienced teacher needs to spend more time in preparation to ensure they get it right in the areas of content, methodology, resourcing and classroom control.

☺ Spend a minimum of 15 minutes per hour of teaching time in preparing lessons.

☺ Plan lessons with a clear step by step structure.

☺ Identify and write down the intended learning objectives.

☺ Organise appropriate resources before the lesson is started.

☺ Anticipate the likely problems which may arise.

☺ Discuss with colleagues other ways of teaching the same concepts, skills and content.

☺ Complete a breakdown of time for the lesson.

☺ Select an appropriate location for the lesson to take place.

☺ List the needs of all students and revise them each term.

☺ Check that you have considered the needs of all students.

☺ Consider the cultural backgrounds of the students so as not to offend their beliefs or values during the lesson.

☺ Determine the prior level of knowledge the students 'should' and do have.

☺ Identify the best motivational learning techniques for the lesson.

☺ Research the key content, skills and concepts to be taught.

☺ Document the key components of the lesson including the teaching strategies and resources you intend to use.

☺ Run off enough worksheets/handouts before the lesson commences.

☺ Check to see if enough materials are available to run the lesson.

☺ Inform students of equipment they will need for the lesson well in advance of the lesson commencing - at least two days before.

☺ Ensure all safety requirements are dealt with during preparation.

THE BEST LAID PLANS OF MICE AND MEN

How much have you changed in your classroom teaching practise in order to adopt the main thrust of the School Development or Strategic Plan of the school?

Observation confirms that the intention of many plans and what transpires at the "chalkface" may be, in many schools, a long way apart.

To implement the plan requires a sound framework and a commitment from staff. Carrying out these actions will go a long way towards bridging the gap.

☺ Make yourself familiar with the School's Strategic and Development Plans.

☺ Analyse the implementation strategies for each priority area.

☺ Blend your own teaching program into the School Plan to reflect priority focus areas.

☺ Measure the effectiveness of your teaching program to provide information for Management Information Systems related to the School Plans.

☺ Allocate resources to support priority focus areas.

☺ Inform parents of your intention of putting an emphasis into the school plan priority areas.

☺ Assure parents that all other areas will not be neglected and that maintenance programs are always operating.

☺ Seek professional development in priority focus areas to enhance your teaching skills.

☺ Make adjustments to your teaching routine and timetable to ensure priority focus areas are being addressed.

☺ Provide feedback and support to the priority focus area planning group.

☺ Engage in educational debates about better ways of implementing priority focus areas.

☺ Demonstrate enthusiasm in the implementation of high priority focus areas.

☺ Request assistance in areas of need or uncertainty.

☺ Make changes to your teaching methodology to reflect the philosophy of the School Plan.

☺ Involve yourself in the School Planning process.

☺ Meet timelines related to the School Plan.

☺ Agree with colleagues that you will implement the plan.

HERE'S HOW WE WANT IT DONE

Policy provides a firm set of parameters by which we can operate. Quite often the policy is supported by a set of guidelines which provides the rationale behind it. These guidelines also provide the detail that help with policy implementation.

When we develop policy it must be relevant, current, valid, practical, acceptable to the stakeholders and able to be resourced adequately.

As with many other areas, consultation with informed stakeholders is crucial to the policy development process. You may find the following of value when next establishing meaningful school policy.

☺ Ensure the planned policy is relevant to the needs of the school.

☺ Inform staff of the reasons for the policy development.

☺ Form a reference group.

☺ Identify key issues related to the policy development.

☺ Identify stakeholders likely to be affected by the policy.

☺ Discuss policy issues with stakeholders.

☺ Prepare a draft policy document.

☺ Establish a consultation strategy after the draft has been written.

☺ Ask for feedback on draft policy.

☺ Establish the clear purpose of the policy.

☺ Write guidelines which clarify policy.

☺ Check that policy is clear, unambiguous and concise.

☺ Determine a policy format which is consistent with the format of other school policies.

☺ Consult with informed staff during the policy development process.

☺ Identify procedures which need to be developed as part of the policy.

☺ Consider the need to be flexible in 'exception to the rule' situations.

☺ Consider statutory requirements during policy formulation.

☺ Establish regular communication briefs.

☺ Establish an implementation strategy.

☺ Inform all stakeholders of the final policy statement.

IS ROUGH ENOUGH GOOD ENOUGH?

Presentation skills are about expectations and standards. For those students who are not naturally neat, trying to present work of a high standard is somewhat of a trauma.

We make a lot of assumptions, as teachers, about the capabilities of students when it comes to the presentation of their work. Many presentation skills are taught at home and too few are taught at school.

Presentation standards of work will improve once you give some serious consideration to your role in the teaching of standards.

☺ Discuss with students the reasons why neat and attractive presentation is important.

☺ Provide examples of the desired standards you are asking of the students.

☺ Provide enough time for the students to complete the work in the manner you expect.

☺ Teach students printing techniques.

☺ Encourage students to learn from students who are skilled in this area.

☺ Provide the necessary materials which will enable the student to improve their presentation.

☺ Allow time to practise the setting out you require.

☺ Model the standards of presentation you expect.

☺ Provide incentives for high standards of work presentation.

☺ Provide hand writing lessons for students whose writing is illegible.

☺ Liaise with other teachers to support your endeavour to lift standards.

☺ Acknowledge and accept the fact that some students are neater than others.

☺ Prepare guidelines as to how you expect students to present their work.

☺ Reward and recognise students who present work of a high standard.

☺ Encourage students to utilise their home computers to assist with presentation eg word processing, graphs etc

☺ Encourage students to use graphs, diagrams, tables, charts, drawings, photographs, maps, etc to accompany text.

LOOK BEFORE YOU LEAP!

The most common failing in decision making is to jump to the first obvious solution. To "do it now!" is a commendable philosophy, but only after the desired outcome is very clear.

A method that effective administrators can use applies equally in any setting which involves people, a specific outcome, and a range of options.

Be very clear on what the desired outcome is in terms of quantity, quality, time frame, costs and so on. Don't worry about actions at this stage, just get a clear picture of what things should look like **after** action has been taken.

☺ Use a step by step problem solving approach.

☺ Analyse the situation before making a decision.

☺ Identify the symptoms then the root causes.

☺ Establish the what, how, when and why of the matter.

☺ Ensure that staff agree with the identification of core issues.

☺ Consider the "hidden" issues as well as the more obvious information.

☺ Seek opinions from staff before making a decision.

☺ Identify all the stakeholders affected by a decision and the consequences of the decision on each stakeholder.

☺ Brainstorm ideas for identifying and solving the problem.

☺ Identify and consider several solutions to the problem.

☺ Identify the consequences of each solution on the school.

☺ Look at the positives and negatives of making the final decision.

☺ Check that your decision is based on the real facts.

☺ Plan how the decision will be implemented.

☺ Communicate your decision and your rationale to other stakeholders.

☺ Budget for implementation of the final decision.

☺ Implement the decision made.

☺ Check to ensure the original problem was solved.

THREE FIFTHS OF FIVE EIGHTHS

Everything we teach should at some stage be placed in the context of solving a problem. Mathematically, we can isolate the numbers and find an answer in the pure sense. In reality, the numbers fit into a problematical framework.

Problem solving is about developing strategies, gathering information, applying rules, carrying out investigations, offering alternatives and analysing the parts that make the whole. It is also about applying the skills and knowledge that have been learnt.

Many schools are putting more emphasis on problem solving. However we don't spend **enough** time teaching students the necessary skills to effectively solve problems.

☺ Explain that problem solving is a sequential process.

☺ Present the problem by reading it aloud to the students.

☺ Identify what it is that needs to be solved, ie desired outcome.

☺ Brainstorm ideas which may assist in solving the problem.

☺ Encourage the students to discuss the problem with each other.

☺ Ensure students make notes about their ideas and findings.

☺ Determine the number of parts to the problem.

☺ Encourage students to explore different approaches to solve a problem.

☺ Encourage students to share their method of solving the problem.

☺ Demonstrate different ways of finding a solution.

☺ Provide resources needed to assist in solving the problem.

☺ Decide on a reasonable time to solve problems.

☺ Begin the teaching of problem solving by providing easy problems first.

☺ Work through similar type examples to model problem solving techniques.

☺ Provide students with realistic and purposeful problems to solve.

☺ Use problem solving to teach, consolidate and complement other concepts.

☺ Assist students with reading difficulties.

☺ Discuss with students that failure is a part of problem solving and is acceptable.

EVERY CALLING IS GREAT WHEN GREATLY PURSUED

If teachers are to be considered true professionals they must take it upon themselves to proactively seek professional development.

Other professions must comply with minimum yearly requirements as set by their professional associations and legislation. They are involved in professional development in their own time and certainly require the support of the organisation for which they work.

Whilst it may be argued that other professions are far better paid than teachers and hence can afford expensive conference type professional development there are many other things you can do to better yourself.

☺ Read literature related to school and teaching issues.

☺ Involve yourself in professional organisations, associations, committees or groups focussing on specific curriculum or professional areas.

☺ Engender enthusiasm about particularly relevant professional development activities to colleagues.

☺ Explore all available options to meet and satisfy your professional development needs.

☺ Budget to enable professional development to take place.

☺ Participate in external courses related to teaching.

☺ Seek the assistance of external organisations to demonstrate the types of teaching strategies in which you may be deficient.

☺ Involve yourself in whole school professional development initiatives.

☺ Promote the need for professional development to parent and community groups.

☺ Ask colleagues which areas they consider are your key professional development needs.

☺ Establish an area of specific expertise in which you can become an authority.

☺ Involve yourself in developing your colleagues by acting as a mentor in areas in which you have expertise.

☺ Attend professional development courses which address areas of personal need.

☺ Organise and facilitate professional development sessions.

☺ Engage in educational debate with colleagues, friends and family.

☺ Ask yourself each term what did I do which was new, different and better than last term.

WE MUST KEEP TOPPING UP THE WELL

The reason we need to maintain a constant involvement in professional development is to:

- learn new strategies
- discover changes
- review different ways to enhance our effectiveness

It is a worry some teachers still teach not just as they did when they first started teaching some 30 years ago, but teach as they were taught. The world has changed around them and is expecting an end product which can meet the needs of the modern business world.

It is our professional duty to ensure that we are updating the skills and knowledge of all staff at every opportunity.

- ☺ Identify the specific professional development and training needs of staff.
- ☺ Discuss with staff your thoughts about their professional development needs.
- ☺ Prepare a yearly staff professional and personal development plan.
- ☺ Promote and inform staff of forthcoming professional development programs.
- ☺ Follow your prepared professional development plan.
- ☺ Budget for future professional development and training needs.
- ☺ Encourage staff to involve themselves in developing their colleagues as mentors.
- ☺ Encourage staff to establish an area of specific expertise in which they can become an authority.
- ☺ Establish professional development and training priorities for staff which link into the school strategic plan.
- ☺ Reward and acknowledge staff who develop their skills.
- ☺ Identify the multi-skilling needs of staff.
- ☺ Build these multi-skilling needs into the professional development plan.
- ☺ Provide coaching and mentoring to staff.
- ☺ Provide quality "off-the-job" professional development training programs.
- ☺ Discuss, prior to their involvement, why staff are being professionally developed and what is expected of them.
- ☺ After professional development and training ask staff how they will apply their new skills and knowledge.
- ☺ Provide ongoing refresher courses relating to subject knowledge.
- ☺ Report back to staff and colleagues your experiences and learnings from any professional development in which you have been involved.

THROUGH THE EYES OF OTHERS

Now here's a tough one.

What is professionalism? A question which could be debated forever. The slant taken in this article reflects the majority of the population's point of view.

This article is aimed at the 5% who, in one way or another, do not meet "professional" standards. Be it in their appearance or the quality of pedagogical practice they undertake.

It's a difficult one to manage because it all boils down to individual perceptions about what might constitute professionalism and how much we value the individual ingredients which make up the professional "cake".

☺ Present yourself in a neat and tidy manner.

☺ Ensure your clothes are clean and ironed.

☺ Wear clothing appropriate to the teaching activity you are performing.

☺ Wear shoes.

☺ Model the image you want your students to follow.

☺ Encourage students to comply with the school dress codes.

☺ Prepare your lessons.

☺ Involve yourself in school activities.

☺ Involve yourself in school community activities.

☺ Demonstrate politeness.

☺ Speak clearly, confidently and correctly.

☺ Write legibly, expressively and correctly.

☺ Comply with school and departmental policies.

☺ Question policies which you believe need to change.

☺ Engage in educational debate.

☺ Arrive at school on time as to the agreed standard.

☺ Communicate with the parents of your students.

☺ Engage in professional development activities.

☺ Mark all student work.

☺ Plan what you intend to teach.

☺ Present a united front to the "customer".

☺ Demonstrate school loyalty.

☺ Involve yourself with school education committees.

☺ Join professional associations.

IDLE MINDS ARE THE DEVIL'S PLAYGROUND

The great majority of school behaviour problems surface during recess and break times. With careful planning and a little thought most of these problems will disappear. Some form of structured activity can keep students meaningfully active.

Remember though, if we are to provide structured activities during the break time, we must ensure that we allow enough interaction, relaxation, recreation and "letting off steam" time to the students. Kids do need some time to themselves.

With positive encouragement from staff some very successful recreational learning programs can be implemented.

☺ Establish set play areas for specific year groups.

☺ Show each year group their designated play and recreation areas.

☺ Establish a roster of activities for students to do.

☺ Provide a group of passive and active activities in which children may be interested.

☺ Show / teach students how to do the activities.

☺ Utilise existing staff expertise to assist with running these activities.

☺ Ask parents or community members with expertise to help supervise activities.

☺ Document the materials and rules relevant to each activity.

☺ Link recess activities to current school themes and activities.

☺ Establish clubs which meet during recess times.

☺ Roster staff as a part of their normal duty to coordinate activities.

☺ Run competitions within nominated activities to stimulate interest.

☺ Reward and encourage students who involve themselves.

☺ Ask students to suggest the type of activities in which they may wish to be involved.

☺ Involve students in the setting up and rostering of activities

☺ Discuss with staff the importance of students being occupied during their break times.

ASK ME NO QUESTIONS AND
I'LL TELL YOU NO LIES

A manager of an organisation was once asked, "How do you know if you're doing a good job?" His response was, "If I'm not getting a kick in the pants then things must be okay."

It was a throw away comment but unfortunately reflects the way many managers manage. The school situation is no different. Many school administrators do not provide any recognition of performance or constructive feedback to staff about how they are going.

It is the responsibility of all school administrators to manage the performance of their staff. A key part of that process is to provide feedback and initiate discussions about performance.

☺ Identify the expectations and perceptions of staff concerning the degree of recognition and feedback they receive.

☺ Ask staff to suggest ways to provide recognition and feedback.

☺ Conduct regular recognition and feedback meetings.

☺ Look for opportunities to acknowledge the good performance of staff.

☺ Identify the aspects of their job that each person does well.

☺ Identify the aspects of their job that each person could improve.

☺ Provide each person with regular feedback covering things done well and things to improve.

☺ Acknowledge "right efforts" as much as "right results".

☺ Seek regular feedback on your own performance.

☺ Make provision for rewards and recognition to be given.

☺ Praise in public, criticise in private.

☺ Direct feedback toward behaviour which the other person can do something about.

☺ Describe the actual behaviour rather than evaluating it when giving feedback on performance.

☺ Maintain a balance between positive and negative feedback.

☺ Check to see that the message (about performance) was received as intended.

☺ Give feedback at the earliest opportunity about the particular behaviour to be addressed.

☺ Take into account the needs of the person receiving feedback.

☺ Discuss and agree standards of performance in key areas.

☺ Discuss the concept of performance indicators.

OFF THE RECORD

Records, records, records! A necessary chore and something which many of us abhor. Like many other things in teaching, keeping records is a discipline that has to be adhered to.

Whatever you do in the way of keeping records - if they're not functional and purposeful then you are wasting your time.

We keep records so that we can provide verifiable evidence about the performance of our students. They are also part of the accountability chain. More importantly, though, we use them to assist us in evaluating our teaching effectiveness.

Well kept records can also significantly simplify the reporting process.

☺ Keep current records of all student test and exam results.

☺ Keep current records of student assignment work.

☺ Maintain records which are relevant to student progress.

☺ Establish a recording system which allows you to locate information quickly.

☺ Use your records to analyse student work to determine the key points of error for individuals.

☺ Use your statistical analysis to guide your teaching.

☺ Analyse student work to determine areas which may not have been taught properly.

☺ Keep statistics which give consistent scales and gradings for comparisons of results.

☺ Use marking systems which produce reliable and valid results.

☺ Discuss with colleagues ways to improve record keeping.

☺ Use a variety of types of data gathering strategies.

☺ Discuss with colleagues the concept of developmental learning and how records can be kept to reflect this philosophy.

☺ Use developmental continua to gauge the progress of your students.

☺ Record anecdotal comments about student progress.

☺ Record standardised test results.

☺ Keep records which can be translated and transposed easily into the school reporting format.

☺ Analyse the effectiveness of your record keeping as to its purpose, function and need.

YOU CAN'T BUY RESPECT

Why are some people more respected than others? What do they do that sets them apart? Two of the qualities they possess are a greater awareness of where they fit into the big picture and an awareness about themselves as individuals. They have no pretences!

We can respect people for the many individual qualities they possess be it their determination, intelligence or just plain kindness. To be respected as a whole person is the ultimate and reflects a combination of special qualities.

We can develop the respect of students quite simply and without compromising our values by performing some of the many actions identified here.

☺ Actively listen to what students are telling you.

☺ Ask students about how they are feeling.

☺ Demonstrate an understanding of their 'culture'.

☺ Seek feedback from students as to what their perceptions are about an issue.

☺ Present your view point in an objective and factual manner.

☺ Demonstrate a sense of humour. Show that you can laugh at yourself.

☺ Respect the confidentiality of students where sensitive issues are involved.

☺ Avoid losing your temper.

☺ Demonstrate consistency when making judgements and decisions about any issue requiring a resolution.

☺ Demonstrate honesty.

☺ Avoid embarrassing students in front of their peers.

☺ Model the behaviours you wish the students to exhibit.

☺ Do what you say you are going to do.

☺ Know your subject.

☺ Demonstrate loyalty to the school.

☺ Speak positively about the school and other staff.

☺ Recognise and reward students who demonstrate the behaviours the school ethos statement is trying to engender.

☺ Know about the community in which the students live.

A+ or C-, PASS OR FAIL,
THEY NEED TO KNOW

There are many ways to report on the progress that the students are making. Formalised reports are perhaps the most common format. Too often these documents are unclear, subjective, impersonal and inappropriate.

Reports to parents must reflect what has been learnt, progress made, the attitude of the student and the degree of participation the student has had.

The formal report will always hold the key role in communicating to parents. This, together with the right balance of other reporting formats, should provide parents with a clear picture of how their child is performing.

- ☺ Inform parents as to the level of performance their child is achieving.
- ☺ Personalise the reporting information to give an accurate description of performance for each student.
- ☺ Identify specific competencies, on which to report, to give a full performance appraisal.
- ☺ Use the best available reporting procedures.
- ☺ Inform parents of the meaning of the specific categories that exist on report forms.
- ☺ Use a variety of ways of reporting to parents e.g work samples, test packages, interviews, assemblies and formalised reports.
- ☺ Allow parents the opportunity to seek clarification in areas of uncertainty.
- ☺ Present the correct standards of grammar and spelling in written form.
- ☺ Verify comments and marks with your records of student performance.
- ☺ Check your gradings with those of other teachers in the same age/year group.
- ☺ Provide feedback on student performance at regular intervals.
- ☺ Comply with school deadlines to complete reports.
- ☺ Discuss with colleagues ways to improve reporting procedures.
- ☺ Cater for the literacy levels of the parents and/or their ability to read English.
- ☺ Establish procedures to ensure parents receive reports.
- ☺ Keep copies of all information reported to parents.
- ☺ Seek feedback from parents as to the format they find useful.

SCHOOL RESOURCES ARE FOR EVERYONE

Schools spend huge amounts of money resourcing learning programs so that the students will benefit and to make teaching easier and more effective. Much of this money is wasted because resources get lost, stolen, damaged, hoarded or just not used.

The responsibility for managing the resources no doubt rests with the school administration. This is not to say that these duties can't be delegated. There are some crucial things that need to be done to keep 'tabs' on just where those resources are and how they can be distributed to the best advantage of those who need them. The students!

115

- ☺ Establish resource areas for specific programmes.
- ☺ Appoint a resource coordinator / cost centre manager for each resource area.
- ☺ Consult with staff as to their resource needs.
- ☺ Purchase new resources as needed.
- ☺ Repair resources in need of repair.
- ☺ Monitor the condition of existing resources.
- ☺ Keep a record of resources.
- ☺ Budget for the purchase of new resources.
- ☺ Establish resource borrowing procedures.
- ☺ Agree with staff the need to comply with borrowing procedures.
- ☺ Agree with staff the need to return and share resources.
- ☺ Train staff in the established borrowing procedures.
- ☺ Allocate 10 minutes to each staff meeting to discuss issues related to the management of resources.
- ☺ Ensure all resources are returned to the main resource centre when not in use.
- ☺ Collect resources from classrooms at the end of each semester.
- ☺ Encourage staff to share resources.
- ☺ Dispose of resources which are outdated or irreparable.
- ☺ Establish preferred supplier relationships for resource purchases.
- ☺ Ensure resource purchases comply with the School's Developmental Priorities.
- ☺ Show new staff what resources are available.

GIVE ME THE RESOURCES AND I'LL DO THE JOB

"Has anybody seen the ..."

"I didn't know we had one of those".

"If you want anything just go into _____'s room. Anything any good is in there."

Some commonly heard phrases echoing through the corridors and staffrooms of the typical school.

Schools accumulate hundreds of thousands of dollars worth of resources over a period of years. Hard earned money is used to buy them but do we get maximum value from them?

Too often resources are lost, damaged, "unavailable", hidden or untraceable. They are there to help our teaching be more effective. With a little bit of discipline and planning the use of school resources will be greatly enhanced.

☺ Use a variety of appropriate resources to assist in developing or presenting teaching concepts.

☺ Discuss with colleagues the importance of students properly handling teaching resources.

☺ Store resources so that they are accessible to other teachers.

☺ Comply with school tracking/recording systems and procedures.

☺ Return resources on time and to the correct area.

☺ Ensure that students treat resources carefully and with respect.

☺ Offer suggestions as to what sorts of resources need to be purchased.

☺ Operate within budgetary constraints to ensure priority items are acquired.

☺ Ensure resources are returned to main storage areas when not in use.

☺ Ensure resources are properly stored in the classroom.

☺ Learn how to use resources to gain maximum benefit during the teaching session.

☺ Show other staff what resources are available.

☺ Share your knowledge of resource use with other staff members.

☺ Use resources for more than just the purpose for which they were designed.

☺ Become a resource area coordinator.

☺ Spend 15 minutes each week finding out about resources you haven't used before.

☺ Allow students to use the resources and to become the 'teacher'.

NEVER TRUST A SKINNY COOK

In the past, respect went hand in hand with age and position Not so now. The movie "To Sir With Love", whilst tame by today's standards, epitomises how respect can be earned. Consequently we cannot take for granted that the title of "teacher" brings respect.

We must also understand that if we are respected the power of our teaching is greatly enhanced. Therefore it is an extremely valuable teaching ally.

These days we are dealing with a more knowledgeable, more sophisticated and a more precocious generation than has ever preceded it. One common factor remains - they are human and are influenced just the same as those before them. If we are to build a closer relationship there are many things to consider.

- ☺ Spend time together in a non-teaching situation.
- ☺ Identify common areas of interest.
- ☺ Model the required behaviours you expect of students.
- ☺ Involve yourself in school activities.
- ☺ Ask students what things they see as important in their education.
- ☺ Familiarise yourself with the community in which the child lives.
- ☺ Keep a sense of humour and be prepared to laugh at yourself.
- ☺ Demonstrate fairness at all times.
- ☺ Inform students of your expectations of them before embarking on any project.
- ☺ Actively listen to student concerns.
- ☺ Act consistently when dealing with issues related to student teacher conflict.
- ☺ Avoid humiliating (be it praise or criticism) students in front of their peers.
- ☺ Invite the families of students to school functions.
- ☺ Reward students who have acted positively towards the school.
- ☺ Discuss your own personal life with students.
- ☺ Introduce your family to your students should the situation present itself.
- ☺ Discuss and clarify your role as the teacher.
- ☺ Discuss and clarify their role as the student.
- ☺ Encourage students to be accountable for their own behaviour.

DON'T LOOK AT ME ...

How often do we hear "that's not my job" or "I didn't know I was supposed to do that" or "whose job **is** it?"

In each instance it comes back to a lack of clarification of roles.

Life in a school can be far less confusing if we know:

- who should be doing what *and*
- what our responsibilities are

Clarification of responsibilities is a leadership function and should be done in consultation with the stakeholders concerned.

Having roles clearly determined will lessen the time to do things, reduce conflict, increase productivity and reduce stress.

☺ Discuss with colleagues what they think their role is.

☺ Discuss with colleagues the benefits of having roles clearly defined.

☺ Describe the tasks and functions that need to be performed by the position in question.

☺ Allocate tasks in an equitable manner.

☺ Determine the level of authority for each position.

☺ Inform others of the authority level which comes with the position.

☺ Negotiate with all similar positions as to what tasks or functions each should perform.

☺ Agree who performs a function, who is consulted, who is advised of the result, who provides information, who makes the decision.

☺ Document the role for each position.

☺ Inform all stakeholders of the role of other positions.

☺ Seek feedback from the staff member as to their level of understanding of their role.

☺ Review roles on an ongoing basis.

☺ Discuss the importance of the role being carried out with the staff member concerned.

☺ Provide support to the staff member to enable them to perform their role.

THINK SAFETY FIRST, SECOND AND THIRD!

Over the past decade safety has become a huge issue for schools and is continuing to have a huge impact on the way we do things. We have a 'Duty of Care' to ensure the school environment is safe for everyone.

Part of the dilemma for schools is the cost to address many of the 'safety issues' which have been identified. Many of these issues have been around for a long time. The emphasis of blame however has shifted from the individual (to take care) to the organisation (to make it safe.)

Both litigation and legislation are acting as powerful incentives for schools to ensure that the worksite campus is safe. By applying these actions you will meet most of the criteria for a safe school environment.

☺ Appoint a safety officer.

☺ Establish a safety committee involving staff and parents.

☺ Identify and document hazards and areas which are unsafe.

☺ Establish a procedure for dealing with unsafe situations and equipment.

☺ Establish clear criteria by which objective and rational assessment can be made.

☺ Inform staff and students of any safety concern you may have as soon as is practical.

☺ Implement action to restrict use of unsafe areas or things.

☺ Notify the appropriate authority to deal with the issue.

☺ Act immediately to limit danger in emergency situations e.g. bomb scares, fires, snakes, hostage situations.

☺ Establish and document a school evacuation procedure.

☺ Ensure all areas display, in a prominent place, a copy of the evacuation procedure.

☺ Practise and update evacuation procedures regularly.

☺ Discuss with staff the implications of "Duty of Care"

☺ Include specific school safety issues into the everyday teaching program.

☺ Ensure play equipment complies with national safety standards before purchasing it for the school.

☺ Budget for the replacement of equipment which may be becoming unsafe.

☺ Reward and recognise people who are safety conscious.

LOOK FOR THE BUTTERFLY ......
NOT THE GRUB

Self esteem and a positive self image are largely formulated in the home environment. You may ask.... "What can I, as a teacher, do to help improve both of these in the limited school time that I have with the student?" The answer; quite a bit.

Teachers who look for the positives in their students really help with the development of their self esteem. Some students only need a taste of success to start blossoming. Others need some firm foundations built before any growth can take place.

☺ Engage in learning about self esteem.

☺ Discuss with colleagues the concept of self esteem.

☺ Research issues related to the development of self esteem.

☺ Identify which students in your class may need a program to assist with improving their self esteem.

☺ Actively listen to students to gauge their feelings through the attitudes which might be expressed.

☺ Offer to arrange help for students who are obviously having problems in this area.

☺ Look for behaviours which indicate a perceived lack of self worth.

☺ Plan activities which are success oriented.

☺ Plan activities which promote cooperation of all participants.

☺ Provide the opportunity for students with low self esteem to assume leadership roles.

☺ Provide counselling to students with low self esteem.

☺ Discuss with students the impact that teasing and bullying has on others with low self esteem.

☺ Discuss with students the importance of cooperation between class members.

☺ Recognise achievement towards desired behavioural outcomes.

☺ Recognise genuine effort.

☺ Link identified students to the school's pastoral care program.

☺ Make yourself familiar with the child's home environment.

☺ Inform the parents in a sensitive and tactful manner about your concerns.

☺ Involve parents in programs that are being implemented through regular communication and counselling sessions.

☺ Seek assistance from outside professionals where needed.

☺ Inform other staff of your intended intervention strategies.

WHERE DOES THE TIME GO?

We cannot manage time ... but we can manage ourselves.

How often do you find that you have too many things to do and not enough time in which to do them? Up goes the stress level - sleepless nights follow, our tolerance level drops and everyone suffers.

Balancing school life and home life is a difficult thing to do. Both have expectations of us. For those of you who are forever running from point A to point B take time out to look over these pointers. They just might help you.

- ☺ Set aside 15 minutes each day to identify your daily/weekly work requirements.
- ☺ Prioritise your work requirements to ensure that they all get completed in the agreed timeframe.
- ☺ Minimise unwanted interruptions which reduce productivity by setting aside a time where you must not be disturbed.
- ☺ Prepare students for the delegation of duties.
- ☺ Delegate work to others who are willing and able.
- ☺ Organise your class room to ensure ease of location of planning documentation and teaching materials.
- ☺ Remain focused on a particular task to ensure it is completed.
- ☺ Plan to tackle a set task to ensure it is completed to the required standard.
- ☺ Provide for breaks in your work day to optimise your thinking ability.
- ☺ Review the effectiveness of your time management.
- ☺ Ensure you have enough sleep to enable you to cope with your daily work requirements.
- ☺ Participate in exercise and recreation to keep your productivity levels high.
- ☺ Use a diary to plan your time and mark in important events and appointments.
- ☺ Use a daily work pad to plan your work day in detail.
- ☺ Use a term planner to gain an overall picture of your work commitments.
- ☺ Arrive at school with enough time to prepare for your day.
- ☺ Say "no" to others when you do not have enough time to help them.
- ☺ Seek assistance from others when you have too much to do.
- ☺ Give yourself 15 minutes of quiet time to reflect on how your day is going.

WE'RE ALL DIFFERENT

Every school has "pockets" of students who require some form of special assistance. They may be academically gifted, unmotivated, disabled, disadvantaged, constantly failing or showing ability in the arts or sport. Whatever reason we need to provide an opportunity for them to develop and achieve their full potential.

Often it is difficult to meet the needs of all groups. This may be due to limited available resources. However, with careful planning and the cooperation of all the stakeholders involved these special groups can be catered for.

☺ Identify groups requiring special assistance.

☺ Timetable staff to provide the necessary teaching time for groups with special needs.

☺ Use appropriate tests and measuring instruments to give valid and reliable data.

☺ Allocate teaching areas to cater for groups with special needs.

☺ Seek assistance from external groups with specific expertise relevant to group needs.

☺ Use Education Department resources to assist with these groups.

☺ Seek funding to support programs the school intends to implement.

☺ Plan for the implementation of required special needs programs.

☺ Monitor student performance to gauge the effectiveness of programs being provided.

☺ Communicate to parents the special programs that are being provided by the school.

☺ Consult with parents to assist in determining which groups will receive special consideration.

☺ Seek professional development to enable yourself to cater for these groups.

☺ Provide professional development to staff to enable them to cater for the needs of a group.

☺ Develop resources appropriate to these groups.

☺ Inform other staff that these groups will require special consideration.

☺ Discuss with colleagues the rationale behind the selection of these groups for assistance with special needs.

☺ Ensure these groups do not become the focus of negativity by other students.

AS YOU START SO SHALL YOU FINISH

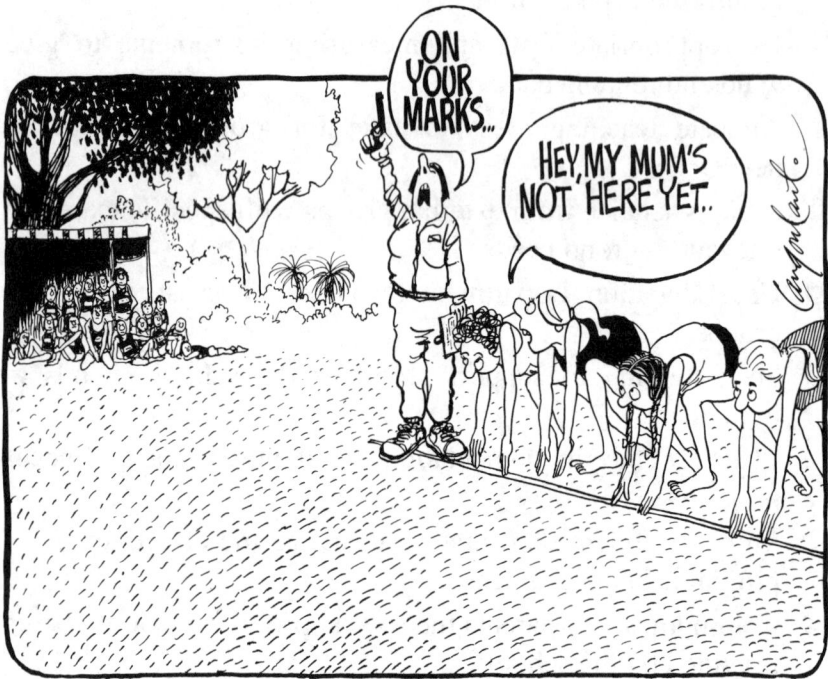

Organising sporting carnivals and events takes a huge amount of time and effort. All too often, we hear complaints from parents, students and other staff because something happened that need not have happened.

It is irritating when the public address system can't be heard or that students wait all day for one event or team events are so close together that they interfere with each other or ...

Too often the organiser doesn't ensure that their organisation is tight enough to prevent criticism. Of course nothing is perfect and you are never going to please all of the people but there are some simple ground rules you need to consider.

☺ Prepare a program which will fit into the school day.

☺ Provide time for students to practise their events.

☺ Allow students to practise their events using similar equipment to that which they will be using on the day of the carnival.

☺ Inform parents of the date and time of the carnival at least four weeks in advance.

☺ Ensure all students are in a minimum of four events.

☺ In the program structure have divisions based on ability.

☺ Include first division events as championship events.

☺ Ensure students and their families know what event they are in before the day of the carnival.

☺ Inform parents of approximate times of events.

☺ Involve parents in judging and setting up.

☺ Involve staff as team coaches.

☺ Provide some form of reward for achievement.

☺ Provide some form of reward for participation.

☺ Ensure the public address system can be heard by both competitors and spectators.

☺ Provide on-going results of individual events and on-going scores of competing teams.

☺ Ensure all team game markings are spaced so that competitors will not interfere with each other during the event.

☺ Provide opportunity for students to practise the start and finish of the event.

☺ Provide shelter from the elements.

☺ Use a finishing tape for flat races.

☺ Inform students of the rules of the events they are in.

☺ Ensure both spectators and competitors have a clear view of the finish line.

☺ Brief all officials as to their roles and duties.

☺ Provide a program for spectators.

NOTHING STAYS UP WITHOUT SUPPORT

One of the key functions of school administrators is to make teaching easier for teachers. Like most disciplines the demands of teaching are changing all the time. There are expectations of teachers which require ongoing change to the way we do things.

If there is an expectation by the school administration for change to take place then a "structure" that will support these changes must be provided. The administration team must should be looking at new, different and better ways of doing things to facilitate this change.

Give some thought to these.

☺ For each new change list the support requirements which are likely to be needed.

☺ Ask staff what support requirements they believe they need.

☺ Ask staff to identify the priority of their support requirements.

☺ Encourage staff to document support requirements.

☺ Provide professional development as a support requirement.

☺ Provide emotional support when a need exists.

☺ Consider the types of support requirements staff may need during the planning stage of any project.

☺ Budget for support requirements.

☺ Offer support in areas you believe staff may need assistance.

☺ Prepare submissions for support from external sources.

☺ Seek assistance from external sources when appropriate.

☺ Make yourself available to support staff and colleagues.

☺ Seek professional assistance for yourself to enable you to provide the support to staff that they may require.

☺ Take into consideration that each individual has different needs for support.

☺ Provide a forum to discuss staff support requirements.

☺ Consider the confidentiality and sensitive nature that some support requirements may have.

☺ Ask colleagues of staff members about situations where support might be needed.

☺ Ask staff to describe what they would like you to do more of or less of to support them.

WE'VE ALWAYS DONE IT THIS WAY

No two schools do things exactly the same way. There are hundreds of systems and procedures which are in place to enable the school to perform its function of "Educational Institution".

Through an evolutionary process systems are "born". They change shape with every 'twist' and 'tweak' and really reflect the culture of the school and the way things are done. We need to review the way we do things when:

- new staff arrive and old staff leave
- our clientele changes
- legislation and policy change
- technology offers new solutions

Never take for granted that because "this is how we've always done it" it is the best way. There are many ways to get the same result. Some ways certainly are more efficient than others.

☺ Identify, define and document key systems used at school.

☺ Define and agree the purpose for all key systems.

☺ Establish and document standard procedures for all key systems.

☺ Discuss standard procedures with staff.

☺ Identify where systems and procedures are not being followed.

☺ Explain systems and procedures to staff.

☺ Identify causes of inefficient systems and procedures.

☺ Identify things we do which seem a waste of time.

☺ Suggest better ways to do things.

☺ Ask the users of our systems and procedures if they can suggest ways to improve them.

☺ Discuss with staff the consequences of their suggestions on all stakeholders.

☺ Consider the impact our systems and procedures have on other parts of the school.

☺ Ask other staff to suggest better ways of doing things in your area/faculty/class.

☺ Discuss with senior school administrators the actions and support you require from them to improve systems and procedures.

☺ Involve staff in discussing how to implement agreed changes to systems and procedures.

☺ Implement agreed changes to systems and procedures.

☺ Implement new systems and procedures.

☺ Acknowledge the efforts of people who act to improve systems and procedures.

☺ Inform staff of the reasons why systems and procedures are to be changed.

☺ Provide ongoing coaching and training to staff in following and implementing systems and procedures.

ART INTO ACTION

Good teachers have an ability to blend the learning ability of the student, the teaching strategy they have chosen, the identified needs of the student and their motivation level into a process which results in a positive learning outcome.

Teaching methodology is about the key ingredients that go into making learning meaningful. It is about encouragement, recognition, feedback, repetition, consolidation, revision, reward, sharing, experience, exploration, discovery, analysis, remediation, enrichment, independence, purpose, development, sequence, monitoring, checking and many other things.

☺ Encourage students to seek clarification in areas of uncertainty.

☺ Use resources to support the current concept or skill being taught.

☺ Cater for the ability level of the students you are teaching by presenting a level of difficulty of concept in which they experience success.

☺ Ask questions to provide for a sharing of knowledge which may already exist.

☺ Ensure the content of the lesson reflects the prior knowledge of the students.

☺ Provide positive feedback to student responses which will encourage them to keep contributing.

☺ Use the abilities and skills of the more capable students to assist in the teaching of less capable students.

☺ Use vocabulary that the students understand - check this.

☺ Ask questions as a means of consolidating a teaching point.

☺ Repeat the key concept being taught.

☺ Get students to take notes about key points.

☺ Provide examples of the concept being taught.

☺ Get students to work through several similar types of problems to consolidate the teaching point.

☺ Provide the answers to problems as soon as is possible after the student has attempted the problem.

☺ Provide recognition of performance at every possible opportunity.

☺ Reward student achievement during teaching sessions.

☺ Reward student effort during teaching sessions.

THERE'S MORE THAN ONE WAY TO SKIN A CAT

Do you still teach the way you were taught when you were at school? Or, do you teach the same things in the same way, year in and year out?

If so, then ask yourself these questions:

> Is it appropriate?
> Is it effective?
> Is it the best way for you?
> Is it the best way for your students?

If the answer to all these questions is a definitive "yes" then keep doing it. If there is any doubt then have a look at these pointers. They might just give you some new and interesting ways to spark up your teaching.

☺ Use learning centres outside the classroom.

☺ Bring outside expertise into the classroom to assist with learning programs.

☺ Set yourself a continual target of one learning strategy each week which is new, different and better.

☺ Budget for activities which may require funding assistance to carry out.

☺ Use existing school resources to assist with teaching activities.

☺ Evaluate the effectiveness of current methods to enable you to continually improve delivery.

☺ Monitor the amount of variety presented to ensure that learning is not disrupted.

☺ Discuss with colleagues about how they present concepts in a different way.

☺ Observe other teachers teaching the same topics.

☺ Engage in professional debate about different ways of teaching.

☺ Arrange for excursions to visit places relevant to the current teaching program.

☺ Ask parents if they have a particular interest or expertise which could assist the learning program.

☺ Use teaching strategies which consider the cultural and ethnic beliefs of students.

☺ Consider the cost factors to individuals when planning teaching excursions or activities.

☺ Develop multi-purpose uses of school resources.

☺ Share your teaching strategies with other staff.

☺ Attend Professional Development courses which address subject specific teaching strategies.

WHY **IS** THE CAPTAIN THE CAPTAIN?

There are some of us who are better leaders than others. What do they do that sets them apart from the pack? Is it a natural set of qualities they possess or can we learn to be better team leaders?

All good captains possess an understanding of the "technical" issues and demonstrate an ability in this area. They also have innate ability to be able to 'rise to the occasion' in times of adversity. More importantly however they manage and understand the 'human' and 'conceptual' issues which influence their team mates.

Here are some very specific things you can do which will help you be a better team leader.

☺ Encourage staff to identify ways to improve team work.

☺ Implement ways to improve team work.

☺ Allow all team members to contribute to decisions.

☺ Identify team members strengths and utilise these to the benefit of the whole team.

☺ Seek regular feedback from team members about your actions.

☺ Clarify the role and authority of each member of the team.

☺ Convey unpopular decisions to the team which result in acceptance without divisiveness.

☺ Establish clear team goals with all team members.

☺ Discuss the benefits of staff working together as a team.

☺ Provide clear direction to the team.

☺ Provide support for the team.

☺ Ensure that communication within the team is accurate, timely and relevant.

☺ Act to resolve any conflict within the team.

☺ Provide feedback on team results.

☺ Provide support for team objectives and activities.

☺ Speak positively about the team.

☺ Avoid asking team members to do things you wouldn't do yourself.

☺ Demonstrate the types of behaviours you wish team members to adopt.

☺ Implement new, better and different ways to improve team work.

☺ Demonstrate consistency when handling team issues.

☺ Discuss team successes and the contributions of team members.

☺ Recognise and reward outstanding teamwork.

KNOW THYSELF

Teamwork within the school environment can always do with improvement. It is mystifying how unaware some people are of the effect they have on others and the team in general.

In most cases people really believe they are good team members. Most team leaders think likewise. One of the most important tasks team members can perform is to assess what they say and do to assist the team to function.

Here is a list of actions you can use to measure the effectiveness of your contribution to the team.

☺ Offer constructive comments to the team rather than destructive comments.

☺ Allow other team members to present a point of view.

☺ Share your ideas with the team.

☺ Contribute to the team without having to be asked.

☺ Look for things to assist others when your workload is quiet.

☺ Offer to do tasks even though you don't enjoy doing them.

☺ Encourage others to contribute towards identifying areas of need for improving teamwork.

☺ Ensure your work is completed to enable the team to function.

☺ Provide assistance when other team members are under pressure.

☺ Tolerate other colleagues deficiencies.

☺ Provide support to colleagues to enable them to overcome their deficiencies.

☺ Keep a sense of humour when things become tense.

☺ Recognise and thank colleagues who have helped you in a time of need.

☺ Think through the consequences of your actions or comments on workmates, before acting or speaking.

☺ Empathise with colleagues who may be having difficulty.

☺ Identify the hidden issues that may be causing people to behave the way they do.

☺ Implement ways to improve teamwork.

☺ Clarify your role within the team.

☺ Clarify the role of others within the team

☺ Act to assist others to implement common goals.

☺ Accept decisions that you may not have agreed with.

☺ Offer encouragement to team members.

☺ Provide constructive feedback on team results.

LIKE IT OR LUMP IT

Technology studies is a curriculum area which is an all encompassing process providing very sound teaching and learning strategies. It should focus on experimentation, exploration, evaluation, analysis, modification, questioning and play.

It is about providing 1) an environment in which these things can happen and 2) a facilitator to ensure that meaningful learning takes place.

Because of its relative newness to the 'curriculum' area many teachers have misconceptions about what technology studies is really all about. Once you understand the real purpose then the student's ability to learn is greatly enhanced.

- ☺ Engage in educational debate about technology.
- ☺ Establish a technology resource area.
- ☺ Appoint a staff representative from each of the traditional subject areas to a technology reference group.
- ☺ Ensure staff understand why technology is being taught.
- ☺ Provide documentation / literature about technology to staff.
- ☺ Identify and document the goals and objectives of technology studies.
- ☺ Match similar objectives from other subject areas.
- ☺ Encourage staff to experiment with technology studies.
- ☺ Timetable all students to receive a minimum of one hour per week.
- ☺ Attend seminars, conferences and professional development courses related to technology.
- ☺ Invite outside expertise into the school to teach technology studies.
- ☺ Seek feedback from students as to the effectiveness of the program.
- ☺ Identify problem areas in the technology program.
- ☺ Seek feedback from staff as to the effectiveness of the program.
- ☺ Prepare a technology studies implementation timeline.
- ☺ Appoint a Technology Studies Coordinator / Teacher in Charge / Cost Centre Manager.
- ☺ Train all staff in how to build technology studies into their subject areas.
- ☺ Write sample lesson plans for each subject area.
- ☺ Inform parents of what and why technology studies is being taught.
- ☺ Allocate a technology studies budget.

WHAT, WHEN AND WHERE

Effective timetabling is about - ensuring all curriculum areas get a 'look in', continuity of teaching takes place, teaching time - blocks cater to the group's learning capabilities, proper utilisation of the expertise within the school and allowing enough time for planning and preparation to take place.

These days there seems to be more and more things to fit into the daily timetable. New subjects, new programs and the like. To ensure the right balance we need to consider many variables to come up with the 'perfect' timetable.

☺ Check to see that all subjects are taught for the recommended time range.

☺ Identify and select the most appropriate times to teach subjects.

☺ Accept that the timetable needs to be flexible to cater for changing circumstances.

☺ Ensure that the time allocated to each subject is long enough to cover the required activity/content of the lesson.

☺ Timetable support and specialist staff who may be available.

☺ Consult with other staff as to the impact your timetabling requirements have on them.

☺ Consider whole school timetabled non-negotiable times ie assembly, special events.

☺ Display the timetable for all users to see.

☺ Allow for continuity of teaching time.

☺ Use available teaching areas to enhance the teaching program.

☺ Provide a copy of the timetable to the school administration, staff and students.

☺ Negotiate with all stakeholders changes which need to be made.

☺ Inform stakeholders of changes to the timetable.

☺ Inform stakeholders of the reasons for the changes.

☺ Inform new staff as to the "history" of the current timetable.

☺ Consider the needs of the whole school as well as the perceived needs of the individual.

☺ Acknowledge that because you've always done it that way that it may not be the best way.

YOU CAN'T TEACH VALUES
OR CAN YOU?

THERE ARE SOME PARENTS HERE WHO WOULD LIKE TO DISCUSS WITH YOU YOUR TEACHING OF VALUES...

Establishing and implementing school values statements is about finding common ground between different cultures, religions and social groups which exist within the school community. You may be surprised just how many common values actually exist once serious attention is given to finding them.

Rather than teach this as another subject, we need to somehow work it into the existing curriculum. With careful planning and thought, 'values' can be shaped around the student.

There is no doubt that this particular topic will be the basis for much discussion. Here are some points of reference as a 'starter' to the process.

☺ Identify subject areas which incorporate values.

☺ Identify key objectives which reflect values.

☺ Model the values that are important to the school.

☺ Acknowledge and reward students who display the values important to the school.

☺ Identify school policies which depend upon school values to be successful.

☺ Discuss the meaning of values with staff and parents.

☺ Inform parents and students as to what the school's values are.

☺ Discuss values which are deemed important.

☺ Focus on small parts of the values education at any one time.

☺ Describe each value as a list of actions.

☺ Identify a values Outcome Area for each lesson presented in the form of a specific objective.

☺ Identify areas where we are already "teaching" the identified values.

☺ Clarify what the term "values" means.

☺ Define and document the meaning of each term.

☺ Select and present literature, videos, music which provide examples of each desired value.

☺ Consider how gender, religion and culture may influence the acceptance of identified values.

☺ Engage in educational debate about Values Education.

THE M•A•P•P™ (EDUCATION) SYSTEM

Steve Godden is the developer of the M•A•P•P™ (Education) System.

This is a process which improves any aspect of school performance through active involvement of all teaching, non-teaching and administrative staff.

It focusses on the development of:

- The School
- The Leader
- The Professional
- The Person
- The Student

It involves:

- Industrial Democracy Principles
- Consultation at All Levels
- Ownership at All Levels
- Verifiable Evidence of Improvements.

For more information phone:

Sydney:	02 9953 7041 (Gael Oswald)
Melbourne:	03 9455 2400 (Joy Bernard)
Perth:	08 9386 8776 (Steve Godden)

Bentley Kehoe Consulting Group also provides the following services to schools:

- Team Building
- School and Customer Surveys
- Strategic and School Development Planning
- Training and Professional Development Programs
- Recruitment - Teachers and Administrators
- Continuous Improvement Systems
- Performance Management Systems
- Quality Assurance